Exploring Hidden
MUSKOKA

Exploring Hidden
MUSKOKA

Andrew Hind

The Publisher: Folklore Publishing
Website: www.folklorepublishing.com

Library and Archives Canada Cataloguing in Publication

Title: Exploring hidden Muskoka / Andrew Hind.
Other titles: Muskoka
Names: Hind, Andrew, author.
Description: Includes bibliographical references.
Identifiers: Canadiana (print) 20200234897 | Canadiana (ebook) 20200235168 | ISBN
9781773110004 (softcover) | ISBN 9781773110011 (epub)
Subjects: LCSH: Muskoka (Ont. : District municipality)—Guidebooks. | LCGFT:
Guidebooks.
Classification: LCC FC3095.M88 H56 2020 | DDC 971.3/16—dc23

Project Director: Faye Boer
Editor: Ashley Bilodeau
Proofreader: Faye Boer
Designer: Tamara Hartson
Maps: Tamara Hartson
Front Cover Image: GettyImages/jimfeng
Back Cover Image: GettyImages/SHSPhotography
Photo Credits: Author's collection, 18, 21, 22, 23, 24, 25, 33, 36, 42, 48, 52, 62, 68, 70,
82, 84, 86, 94, 96, 99, 104, 108, 128, 136, 150, 152, 156, 160, 162, 166, 168, 178, 182,
190, 194, 196, 197, 198, 205. 178. Albion Arts, 17; Balas Museum Archives, 26;
Bethune Memorial House National Historic Site, 140, 143; Bigwin Golf and Country
Club, 30; Brooklands Farm, 38; Carol Fraser, 192; Chancery Lane Court House, 80;
Clevelands House, 45; Clublink, 186; Clyffe House Cottage Resort, 46, 47; Deerhurst
Resort, 3, 50; Dorset Heritage Museum, 54; Ginny Ball, 116, 144, 164; Gravenhurst
Archives, 16; Gravenhurst Opera House, 74; Hilltop Interiors, 90; Ian Turnbull, 64;
JW Marriott The Rosseau Muskoka Resort, 148; Larry Wright, 114; Muskoka
Conservancy, 60; Muskoka Discovery Centre, 185; Muskoka Heritage Place, 154;
Muskoka Lakes Farm and Winery, 124; Muskoka Lakes Museum, 158; Muskoka
Tourism, 58; Nancy Tapley, 146; Ron Sclater, 206, 209; Rosseau Historical Society, 92,
100, 170, 172, 174, 177; Samantha Lee (@wanderingtides), 106; Sherwood Inn, 189;
Town of Bracebridge, 34, 78, 88, 200, 210; Town of Gravenhurst, 72; Town of
Huntsville, 40, 120, 132, 135; Township of Algonquin Highlands, 56; Windermere
House, 202. Wikimedia Commons: Hans-Jürgen Hübner, 118; P199, 112.

Produced with the assistance of the Government of Alberta. *Alberta*
                                                           Government

We acknowledge the financial support of the Government of Canada.
Nous reconnaissons l'appui financier du gouvernement du Canada.

Funded by the Government of Canada | Canadä
Financé par le gouvernement du Canada

PC: 29-1

Dedication

This book is dedicated to my parents, Murray and Wendy, who sacrificed so much so that we could have a cottage upbringing.

Acknowledgements

I have to begin with a shout out to tourism stakeholders past and present—those who laid the foundation of Muskoka as being one of Canada's premier vacation destinations and those who proudly carry on this mantle into the 21st century.

I am grateful to the many folks who encouraged and assisted me throughout the process of writing this book, especially Lauren MacDermid (Town of Huntsville), Sarah Tauro (JW Marriott The Rosseau Resort), Doug Smith (Muskoka Lakes Museum), Judy Humphries (Gravenhurst Archives), Jill Taylor (Town of Bracbridge), Krista Storey (Gravenhurst Opera House), Kelly Collard (Rosseau Historical Society) and Katie O'Hearn (Muskoka Tourism).

And my thanks to Faye Boer, for seeing the potential in this project, and the rest of the hard-working crew at Folklore Publishing—especially, but not limited to my editor, Ashley Bilodeau.

Last, but not least: My undying love to my wife and daughter, who are so understanding when Daddy steps into his office and vanishes into history.

Contents

Prologue

Beautiful wilderness and rustic communities alongside luxurious resorts and comfortable cottages—Muskoka is an unforgettable destination, and there's no better way to get to know this diverse region than by hitting the road. So fill up the gas tank, pack a lunch, and buckle up.

Exploring Hidden Muskoka takes you through the Muskoka we know today and the Muskoka that has been. Many of the region's interesting sights have roots deeply planted in the past, which is why each location in this book was selected for both its rich history and its appeal today.

Whether you want to explore the rural backroads or spend the day in Muskoka's larger communities, or whether you're on the hunt for heritage-filled museums, family-friendly attractions or that perfect place to rest your head, this book has got you covered.

Turn the page to discover idyllic landscapes of green and blue, soothing resorts and charming villages and towns in one of Canada's most iconic regions. With this book as your travel companion, you can explore the countless sights that make Muskoka a unique destination.

Note: This book is not a comprehensive travel guide to Muskoka. A book listing every stop-worthy restaurant, attraction, shop and hotel would be immense. For more information when planning your trip, turn to Muskoka Tourism and Explorer's Edge. Both will prove invaluable.

Muskoka Tourism (www.discovermuskoka.ca)
Explorer's Edge (www.explorersedge.ca)

A Brief History of Muskoka

As late as the mid-19th century, Muskoka remained a remote and unsettled wilderness. First Nations called the region home, and the occasional trapper endured the months of solitude to earn a meagre living, but there was little incentive for homesteaders to press into this expanse of impenetrable forests.

But Muskoka's numerous pine stands were too tempting to ignore for long. As forests in the settled southern portions of Ontario were exhausted of harvestable timber, lumber companies became increasingly anxious to gain access to the region's valuable timber. There was an impediment to their plans, however: the lack of permanent inhabitants and infrastructure in the region made it difficult to exploit these resources.

Heeding to the calls of the lumber industry, the government of Ontario passed the Free Grants and Homesteads Act in 1868. Under this plan, the government offered 100 acres of land to any settler who was prepared to move into the uninhabited north (heads of families had the right to claim 200 acres). The only stipulation was that the settler was expected to clear 15 acres, build a house and live on the site for five years. Over the following decades, thousands would take up the offer, founding farms and villages throughout Muskoka and gradually bringing a sense of civilization to the region.

Sadly, the settlers' dreams of bountiful farms were cruelly crushed. In much of Muskoka, the only thing holding the soil together were the roots of the trees. Once the trees were felled to make room for farm fields, the thin layer of soil covering the Canadian Shield washed away. Even in the best of years, most farms could barely harvest enough to sustain the farmer and his family. Prosperity through tilling the soil and cultivating crops proved elusive, and most farmers took jobs at winter logging camps just to keep their families fed.

Naturally, many settlers became disappointed with their farmland and began to search for other means of making a living. They found they could reap greater success by opening their homes to hunters and fishermen—mostly wealthy and well-born men from the U.S.—who were seeking the adventure of the Canadian wilderness. Soon, these sportsmen were bringing their families to Muskoka to enjoy its natural appeals. Purpose-built resorts were built to cater to them, and the Muskoka tourist industry was born.

By the 1890s, Muskoka had become one of the most popular holiday regions in North America. Though a brief hiccup occurred during World War One, the Golden Era of Muskoka's resorts endured into the 1920s and through the Big Band Era. At the time, the biggest names in music could be found playing in resort dance halls and ballrooms throughout the region. It was a heady time, as the wealthy

flocked to Muskoka each summer to indulge themselves in luxury, dancing, sport and socializing with
their peers.

Muskoka changed forever in the post-World War
Two period. The rise of the middle-class, the spread
of paved highways throughout the north and the
appearance of modern cars in every driveway meant
that is was easier and more affordable than ever
to visit Muskoka. But rather than stay at resorts,
this new breed of vacationer opted to purchase
cottages of their own, and soon the lakes were dotted
with rustic cabins. It became a summer ritual to pack
up the kids every Friday night and make the trip
north for a weekend of relaxation and play. Over
the decades, the cottages have gotten bigger—
multimillion-dollar vacation homes that dwarf their
predecessors in scale and design are the new norm—
but the ritual remains the same.

Some resorts have adapted and thrived and are
once again at the centre of Muskoka's identity. One
of the most beloved tourist destinations in Canada
with a reputation that spans the globe, Muskoka is
arguably more popular than ever. The resorts that
have endured open their doors to these global visitors
with warmth and style, providing comfort for
travelers exploring the region's many delights.

Muskoka has seen a lot of changes since being
opened to settlement, but one thing that has remained
consistent is her natural splendor: small communities and endless expanses of verdant forest speckled

withlakes of crystal-clear waters. The excitement that drove the original settlers to the region remains today, though this energy is not directed toward agricultural pursuits or lumbering, but leisure and relaxation.

Arts at the Albion

100 Muskoka Road N.
No Admission
Web: www.artsatthealbion.com
Email: artsatthealbion@gmail.com
Phone: 705-687-9165

The stunning Albion Hotel has been a fixture in Gravenhurst for more than 130 years, replacing the first Albion that was razed by fire in 1887.

Arts at the Albion makes for a fine pause during any Muskoka road trip. It's worth a peek for its airy galleries of local artwork alone, but also for the opportunity to step inside one of Gravenhurst's most historic structures: the Victorian-era Albion Hotel.

George Washington Taylor, the town's reeve, erected the Albion Hotel at Gravenhurst's main intersection in 1879. Originally a wood frame building, the hotel burned in the great fire of 1887 that razed much of the community. The current structure, with its attractive brickwork, was erected after the fire and became the hub of the community with 25 guest rooms and a large dining room, parlour and bar.

Over the years, numerous colourful stories became embedded within its walls. In the late 19th century, Gravenhurst was at the centre of a vibrant lumbering industry. Booze flowed freely in the bar room and fights were common. One night, two guests staying at the Albion heard a commotion in the streets below. They opened a window to see what was going on and were told by gathered toughs to mind their own business. When they didn't immediately comply, they were chased back inside by several gunshots aimed in their direction.

Things had settled by the time the Albion was declared a historic building in 1983, and the town embarked on a restoration project to preserve the building as an example of Edwardian architecture.

Today, under the banner, Arts at the Albion, the once-hotel hosts a co-op for more than 20 regional artists who have breathed life back into its historic rooms.

Recently renovated, the hotel now houses Arts at the Albion, a co-op for local artists and artisans.

Bala Bay Inn

3063 Highway 169, Bala
Web: www.balabayfoodandspirits.com
Email:balabayfoodnspirits@gmail.com
Phone: 705-762-2222

E.B. Sutton built Muskoka's first brick summer resort, originally named the Swastika Hotel after an ancient symbol of peace and prosperity.

The Bala Bay Inn has a remarkable history. It was the first brick resort in Muskoka, hosting big-band legend, Louis Armstrong, whenever he played at Dunn's Pavilion, and may have been the site of secretive meetings—led by American President, Woodrow Wilson, who cottaged nearby—to stave off World War One.

The founder of the hotel, Ephraim Browning (E.B.) Sutton, moved to Bala in 1899 after an earlier resort he'd founded, Camp Sutton, burned to the ground. A relative of poet Robert Browning and friend of author Charles Dickens, Sutton was a talented artist in his own right, penning a number of popular songs of the day. He built a store in Bala, but his mind would soon turn to running another resort.

When E.B. Sutton built The Bala Bay Inn in 1912, it was called the Swastika Hotel. Before the swastika was corrupted by Adolf Hitler, the swastika had been a symbol of luck and prosperity in numerous cultures dating back millennia. But in the 1930s, as the Nazi party rose to power in Germany and war seemed imminent, the Sutton's changed the name of their hotel to Sutton Manor to distance themselves from hateful connotations. If you look carefully at either end of the hotel facing the lake, you will still see a swastika just below the roofline. Though they have been painted over many times in an effort to disguise them, they remain as a link to the hotel's past.

In fact, the hotel experienced its greatest prosperity during its time as the Swastika. During the 1920s and 30s, it was a prosperous hotel frequented by wealthy patrons. Fortunes dipped after the name change, but today one can still find a number of features hinting at the hotel's earlier grandeur.

Crane your neck in the Ghost Lounge, and you'll see the original tin ceilings—a luxury only the wealthy could afford. At the time, the ceiling would have been painted white to give the illusion of hand-carved or molded plaster. If you look carefully, you can still see holes in the tin ceiling where acetylene gas pipes were fed through to light the hotel. At the time, in the absence of electricity, acetylene was the height of opulence. It was a dangerous novelty; however, as acetylene was highly combustible. Indeed, the neighboring Windsor Hotel burned down as the result of a gas explosion in August 1909. Sutton's decision to build his hotel out of bricks (the first in Muskoka) was an effort to safeguard against such a disaster and reassure his guests.

Other reminders of the Inn's glory days include old rate schedules posted on the walls, sconces for oil lamps, aged pine floors and an inviting pine bar in the bar room. There was much controversy when the beer parlour opened in the late 1940s because when Sutton purchased the land from the previous property owner, he had promised that the inn would never serve alcohol. E.B. Sutton and his son and successor, Fred, faithfully stuck to this promise, but by the 1940s the hotel had been sold and its successors felt no such responsibility. The bar room was male-only for decades. Because it was unseemly to drink with members of the opposite sex in public, women had to drink in another room across the hotel, a room now known as The Ghost Lounge.

The Ghost Lounge is aptly named. It was here that E.B. Sutton was laid in state for a number of days after his death in 1916 in a spot directly opposite the still-standing fireplace. Ever since, stories say the room—indeed, the entire hotel—has been visited by spectral phenomenon.

The most impressive historic feature is undoubtedly the mahogany grand staircase that leads from the lobby up to the second floor. Even a century later, the dark wood still inspires, exuding an aura of class and elegance. Looking at it, you can't help but imagine women who would glide regally down the stairs, the hems of their long dresses brushing against the carpet with an airy rustle.

Even after more than 100 years, the Bala Bay Inn still has her secrets to share. Though she keeps them closely guarded, they can be found... if you know where to look.

Sadly, the building no longer serves as a hotel, but the lobby remains accessible to the public.

No longer a resort, the Bala Bay Inn still stands proudly.

BALA ELECTRIC LIGHT AND POWER COMPANY

River Street, on the shores of Mill Creek, in Bala

Built on the site of town founder Thomas Burgess's sawmill, a hydro generating station began supplying local needs in 1917.

In recent years, the subject of hydroelectricity has been a hot topic in Bala, where, despite local opposition and the objections of environmentalists, an electricity-generating plant has been installed to harness the power of the community's iconic waterfall.

A century ago, the introduction of hydroelectricity was greeted instead with excitement. Back then, everyone in town realized that the proposal would represent an important leap forward for Bala.

The project was the brainchild of Thomas Burgess. Burgess arrived in Bala in 1868, opened a store and post office, and erected a sawmill that ran until 1910.

Burgess founded the Bala Electric Light and Power Company in 1917 and built a generating station on the site of the old mill. Residents of Bala were excited by the possibilities electricity promised, and before the year was out, there were electric lights throughout Bala. Soon, lines extended as far afield as Port Carling and MacTier.

Ontario Hydro took over the generating plant in 1929 and operated it until 1957.

Today, Burgess Generating Station sits idle, an impressive stone monument of a scheme that revolutionized life in Bala.

Note: A plaque commemorating the landmark hydroelectric generating plant is in a parkette at the corner of Highway 169 and River Street.

A plaque marks the Bala hydro achievement.

Bala Falls
Highway 169, Bala

The Falls in Bala have been stirring emotions forever.

All of the water from the watershed of the three big Muskoka lakes, reaching as far afield as Algonquin Park, will eventually flow through Bala Falls on its way to the Moon and Musquash Rivers and then on to Georgian Bay. To say that's a lot of water is an understatement. So while there are bigger waterfalls in Muskoka, and arguably prettier ones, likely none is more significant.

Indeed, the history of the Bala Falls offers a cautionary tale for anyone considering altering its water flow. For millennia, the water levels on Lake Muskoka fluctuated wildly, making it difficult for steamship skippers to reliably know where they could pilot their vessels. After a number of groundings, the Department of Public Works installed a dam above the falls in 1873 to assist in safe navigation. Unfortunately, the dam worked too well and kept water levels too high, swamping lakeside farm fields. As a result, the Department blasted out spillways on the south channel which, in its natural state, had not carried that much water before.

Consequently, there are actually two sets of falls in Bala today: the main outlet, which rushes past the town park, and the spillway, which cascades behind the picturesque Burgess Memorial Church.

Note: Burgess Memorial Church is an attraction in its own right. Built of local stone in 1926, it served Presbyterians for decades. A plaque by the entrance explains that it was built in the memory of town founder Thomas Burgess.

Bala Falls sees Lake Muskoka empty into the Moon River.

Bala's Museum

Admission
Web: www.balasmuseum.com
Email: balamus@muskoka.com
Phone: 705-762-5876

Bala's Museum commemorates *Anne of Green Gables* author Lucy Maud Montgomery's Bala vacation and how it inspired perhaps her finest novel, *The Blue Castle*.

The *Anne of Green Gables* books made author Lucy Maud Montgomery a legend in Canada and one of the world's most-read writers. Millions flock to Prince Edward Island to connect with the author and her famous red-haired character, but you needn't go so far afield. Head instead to Muskoka, the setting for the only one of Montgomery's books not set in PEI. Today it is home to a museum lovingly devoted to everything Lucy Maud Montgomery.

In the summer of 1922, Montgomery and her husband had planned to holiday. It was a sorely needed vacation; Montgomery had been mentally drained from throwing herself so completely into her writing and was physically exhausted from fulfilling the community duties expected of a minister's wife. A rest and change of scenery would surely do her good and perhaps lift her spirits. They settled on Roselawn, a small summer resort in Bala.

Over the next two weeks, she and her family enjoyed a peaceful and thoroughly enjoyable vacation. The family sailed, picnicked, drove along country roads and rode on leisurely boat trips, enjoying the simple pleasures of a Muskoka vacation. Montgomery spent quiet moments reading, editing her manuscripts, doing needlepoint and knitting, looking at views "so lovely they hurt" and fell asleep at night to the music of the cascading Bala Falls. The setting so entranced Montgomery that it inspired her to write *The Blue Castle*, a bestseller which many critics consider to be among her best work.

Roselawn wasn't serving meals at that time, so the Montgomery's ate at Tree Lawn Tourist House, a small boarding house operated by Fanny Pike located just a block away.

Fast forward seven decades. While honeymooning in Prince Edward Island, Linda Hutton—who fell deeply in love with Montgomery's work as a child—and her new husband, Jack, discovered the author's connection to Bala. Soon after their return, they discovered that the former tourist home in Bala where Montgomery and her family had their meals during that holiday might be demolished. Realizing the historic significance of the building, the Hutton's purchased the old home with plans to open a museum celebrating the life and writing of Lucy Maud Montgomery.

The next year was spent restoring the old home to a state which Montgomery might recognize and tracking down vintage books (today, the museum boasts one of the finest collections of first edition Montgomery books in the world), photographs and other relics related to the famed author. One of the prized artifacts is a sterling tea set gifted by the heirs of LMM.

The Museum, officially known as Bala's Museum with Memories of Lucy Maud Montgomery, opened on July 24, 1992, coinciding with the 70th anniversary of the author's coming to Bala. Over the next 20 years, the Huttons and their museum have shared the story of how Bala helped inspire *The Blue Castle* with more than 12,000 visitors. In 2013 the museum received heritage designation from the Township of Muskoka Lakes and, thanks to the international popularity of Anne of Green Gables, is today among Muskoka's premiere attractions.

Tours of the museum blend details of LMM's life and remind us of her most famed works. In the kitchen, authentically restored to the 1920s when Montgomery visited, we're reminded of the scene when Anne finds a mouse dead in the batter because she forgot to cover it with cloth. Elsewhere, a table on the porch set up for a tea service reminds us of the time when Anne gets her "bosom friend" Diana Berry drunk on raspberry cordial. And when we see a rowboat—the rowboat from the Megan Follows television miniseries—we instantly remember the scene when Anne melodramatically replays the "Lady of Shallot."

A highlight is an opportunity to don red-haired pigtails and recreate the iconic scene from the Anne of Green Gables series that sees the orphan sitting on a bench in front of a railway crossing sign, waiting to be picked up by Matthew and wondering if she will have to spend the night in a tree.

Lucy Maud Montgomery considered herself a "word painter" for her livid descriptions. She would have undoubtedly had a beautifully evocative way of describing the appeal of Bala's Museum. But perhaps it's enough to simply say the museum is a loving tribute to one of the world's most beloved authors and a wonderfully entertaining way to connect with the Anne stories we grew up with.

Bigwin Inn

1137-2 Old Highway 117, Baysville
Web: www.bigwinisland.com
Phone: 1-800-840-4036

In its heyday, Hollywood stars, such as Clark Gable, and giants of industry, such as the Rockefellers, patronized Bigwin Inn.

At one time, Bigwin Inn was the toast of Muskoka. Nestled on a private island paradise in the midst of Lake of Bays, it was one of the finest resorts anywhere in North America and patronized by royalty, captains of industry (the Rockefellers and Wrigleys spring to mind), government officials of the highest rank, and Hollywood legends like Clark Gable, Humphrey Bogart, and Carol Lombard.

The visionary behind the resort, Charles Orlando Shaw, was a Huntsville tannery owner who was also a major stakeholder in the Huntsville, Lake of Bays

Navigation Company. Much of the company's business saw its steamships ferrying passengers to resorts across Lake of Bays, so Shaw reasoned business would improve if he built a luxury hotel.

There was also an element of petty vindictiveness involved in the decision. Shaw was a regular at the WaWa Hotel, but one day, when he tried to get a room, he was turned away as the resort was fully booked. Incensed, Shaw vowed not only to never return but also to upstage the WaWa by building a bigger, better hotel of his own on nearby Bigwin Island.

He was true to his word on both counts. He never stepped foot in the WaWa again (it burned to the ground in 1923, with 23 dead) and built a resort that, when it opened in June 1920, surpassed anything yet seen in Muskoka. Indeed, the Bigwin Inn was the largest resort anywhere in the British Commonwealth. It was all style and luxury; women wore gowns and men ties and tails to dinner. The only thing Shaw would not tolerate was alcohol, so the inn was totally dry—at least in public spaces where Shaw and staff might witness drinking.

Bigwin's most identifiable structure, the Indian Head Room, could seat more than 700 people at one time. Twelve-sided in design, this massive room boasted a vaulted ceiling, expansive windows offering spectacular views of the lake, three stone fireplaces and an orchestra gallery. Food was delivered with theatrical synchronicity—waitresses appearing from the kitchens in perfect lines, trays held aloft. When all were in position, the trays were lowered as one.

Among the many luxuries was lawn bowling, croquet, horseback riding, dancing to the tunes of the finest musicians of the Big Band era and, most notably, an 18-hole golf course designed by legendary golf course architect Stanley Thompson. Thompson designed more than 150 courses in his legendary career (among them Windermere Golf and Country Club and, in Port Carling Muskoka, Lakes Golf and Country Club).

Bigwin Inn thrived but began to decline in the years after Shaw's death in 1942. The resort then closed and deteriorated over the decades.

Now, 80 years after it opened, Bigwin's glory days are back. Revived as Bigwin Island Golf Club, it is now an exclusive golf course and recreational community.

The golf course was completely redesigned by Doug Carrick in 2001. While most of the fairways and greens where Gable and Bogart once swung their clubs have been extensively altered, you can still find some of the tee decks—about the size of a table-top and built of Canadian Shield rock to lift them off the greens—in the tree lines. In addition to sensational golf, members enjoy world-class resort amenities and the opportunity to savor a meal in Bigwin Inn's original dining room with its glorious lake vistas.

Bigwin Inn was *the* luxury resort of her day, frequented by Hollywood stars and tycoons.

While Bigwin Island is reserved for members and guests in July and August, it opens its gracious doors to the public in the spring and fall.

Note: Bigwin Island is named after Chief John Big Wind ("Bigwin" being an Anglicized version of the name). The Big Wind family had claimed much of the Lake of Bays region as their ancestral hunting ground. Big Wind and other chiefs relinquished the land in treaties during the 1830s to 1850s and moved to Rama, but Chief Big Wind continued to summer here.

Bracebridge Falls

Located at the Ecclestone Drive-Manitoba Street Bridge, Bracebridge

The stunning beautiful Bracebridge Falls are a popular tourist attraction.

In the 19th century, settlers sought out waterfalls to power their industries and communities inevitably developed around them. Bracebridge is a perfect example; the town grew up around Bracebridge Falls, and this magnificent natural feature remains at the heart of the community to this day.

Bracebridge was still a rough frontier hamlet when Alexander Bailey arrived in 1865 and built a grist mill at the base of the falls. The mill was a godsend. Previously, settlers had to travel to Orillia to have grain milled into flour. At its peak, the Bailey mill was producing 75 barrels of flour per day. Water entered the mill turbine by way of a diversion weir at the edge of the falls, the remains of which can still be seen today. The Bailey mill burned in 1909, but a waterwheel memorial stands on its site.

The most notable industry to harness the power of the falls, however, was the Bird Woollen Mill. Henry Bird established the mill in 1872. Wooden but later bricked over, the three-and-a-half storey mill was the largest industry in town for decades, manufacturing all manner of woollen goods, including mackinaw jackets and blankets that were in high demand by the local logging industry.

A true symbiotic relationship formed between Bird and the settlers: farmers supplied the mill with its wool needs, and in return, the mill ensured a ready market for their goods. As a result, the Bird Mill was vital in sustaining Muskoka's early development.

The Bird Mill thrived for decades, but the decline of Muskoka's logging boom in the 20th century meant a drop in the demand for mackinaw jackets. Worse was the rise of synthetic fibres in the post-war period. Unable to fend off the inevitable any longer, the venerable industry closed in 1954 and was demolished shortly after.

Evidence of the mill remains; however, the mill's foundations are visible on the west side of the river between Bird Mill Bridge and the railway bridge. In addition, the former warehouse still stands alongside the bridge and is now the home of the Bracebridge Chamber of Commerce and a restaurant. When you visit, note the unique stone countertop within the chamber office, which was formerly an altar for the local Society of St. John chapel. Look closely at the corners and centre of the stone, and you'll see carved crosses.

Two hydro generating plants were built at the falls. The original (no longer in operation, but still standing above the falls) dates back to the 1890s when W.S. Shaw built it to supply electricity for his tannery, Anglo-Canadian Leather Company, farther down the river. In 1894, the Town of Bracebridge bought the generating station, making it the first Ontario municipality to own its own power plant. The generating station later became a water-pumping station. The newer plant—an unusually attractive

For 150 years the falls have been behind Bracebridge's prosperity, powering two generating stations and many industries.

structure given its purpose—was built below the falls in 1902, and today it is the oldest continuous operating hydro plant in Canada.

Of course, the falls are the main attraction. A viewing platform, accessed via a trail on the east side of the river above the Manitoba Street-Ecclestone Drive Bridge, provides an excellent vantage point from which to witness the roaring waters. Follow the trail a bit further to view the much smaller 3-metre-high (10-foot-high) upper falls.

Note: Take the time to walk along the trail skirting Bracebridge Bay below the falls and read the various historic markers along the way, most with photos depicting how the location looked in the past.

Brooklands Farm

1375 Butter and Eggs Road
Web: www.brooklandsfarm.ca
Phone: 705-764-1888

The Riley's have been farming Brooklands Farms since 1876 since the land was settled by Charles Riley. It offers a true taste of Muskoka.

Muskoka isn't known for its agriculture. The ever-present rock and trees and the shallow, nutrient-poor soil make it difficult to raise crops, but the region was founded by hardy settlers who replaced forests with fields of swaying hay, golden grain and plump vegetables. One of the few farms to endure from those difficult years is Milford Bay's Brooklands Farm.

Charles Riley began farming on the property that is now Brooklands Farm in October 1876. He was forced to experiment with different animals and crops in an attempt to find a winning combination. Through ingenuity and hard work, he succeeded in establishing a farm that today is run by the fifth generation of the family, Ken and Katya Riley.

Over the years, Brooklands Farm has undergone a number of transitions, from mixed farming under Charles Riley to dairy farming in the early 20th century. Today, the 30-acre property is devoted to market gardening—sweet corn, asparagus and rhubarb grown from stock planted by the family over 100 years ago and six acres of pick-your-own strawberries—as well as a thriving maple syrup operation employing traditional principles and 21st century technology (the maple syrup produced has a distinctive flavor owing to the unique mineral content of the farm's soil).

The farm boasts a number of restored heritage buildings, including a century-old sugar shack, a 1913 barn and the original 19th century log cabin—the latter two frequently used as event venues for weddings and other celebrations.

Brooklands Farm offers a true taste of Muskoka.

Brunel Locks

561 Brunel Road, Huntsville
No Admission

Built in 1875, the Brunel Locks removed a 10-foot waterfall at the foot of Fairy Lake, allowing vessels to sail between Fairy and Mary lakes.

When land-hungry settlers began arriving in the Huntsville region, they found an imposing obstacle to navigation on the Mary-Fairy-Vernon Lake chain: a frothing, 3-metre (10-foot) waterfall and rapids at the end of Fairy Lake.

To enable passage of vessels down to Mary Lake and to open the lake up to industry and settlement, the settlers decided to build a lock and dredge the river. The lock was ready for use in 1875 and was a boon as expected.

The locks still remain, surrounded by an attractive waterside park. At the upper end of the lock chamber, visitors will notice a small swing bridge that seems to lead nowhere. Today the bridge is without purpose, but for almost a century it provided access to the longest operating water-powered sawmill in Muskoka.

In 1873, John Fetterly built a sawmill on the east side of the river, using the swiftly flowing waters of the Muskoka River to power the whirling blades. Fetterly also added a gristmill. While the gristmill was relatively short-lived, the sawmill endured. Steam tugs carried the lumber cut here to Huntsville and places farther afield throughout north Muskoka.

Fetterly sold the mill, and it subsequently changed hands several times before being acquired by the Cottrill family in 1907. The Cottrill's continued sawing lumber and solely using water power to operate the machinery until 1954, well after most mills had first turned to steam and then electricity.

The locks are tranquil today, but if you listen closely as the wind rustles the leaves, you may still hear the echo of this historic sawmill.

Clevelands House

1040 Juddhaven Road, Minett
Web: www.clevelandshouse.com
Email: reservations@clevelandshouse.com
Phone: 705-765-3171

Charles James Minett settled in Muskoka in 1869. His modest farm evolved into one of Muskoka's most famed resorts.

In 1867, 25-year-old Charles James Minett set sail for Canada with his young wife, Fanny. He was the sixth son of a large family and saw no real prospects for himself in Britain, but Canada offered opportunities. Minett lived in Toronto for several years and might have remained largely anonymous had fate not intervened. After contracting a severe case of bronchitis, his physician urged him to move to the healthful, restorative climate of Muskoka. Heeding the advice, the Minetts headed north in 1869.

Charles built a large home, and with room to spare, the Minetts began to take in summer visitors. According to local lore, a pair of English aristocrats, Lord Lambert and Earl Baker, who had travelled to Muskoka to hunt and fish but had gotten snowed in for the winter, were among the earliest guests. They ended up remaining with the Minetts for six months and encouraged Charles to build a hotel.

Charles opened the resort in 1883, and business boomed from the beginning. By 1891, expansions were undertaken, adding a third storey to keep up with demand. Guests arrived by a steamer in the early days, which gave Charles the idea of making his hotel look like a ship (note the octagonal tower that resembled the pilothouse of a very large lake steamer). Unfortunately, while construction was underway, Charles fell and suffered grievous injuries, including broken ribs, which complicated the pneumonia that would claim his life in 1892.

Son Arthur (known to all as S.A.) and his wife Alice took the reins and guided the hotel into a new century. Alice was the face of the hotel, handling all front-of-house operations. Guests rarely saw S.A., who focused most of his energies on making Clevelands House a self-sufficient, though well-managed, farm (oats and corn, for example, were grown in fields where the golf course stands today).

Due to its excellent reputation, the resort saw guests virtually lined up to enjoy a vacation at Clevelands House and every decade or so, it seemed, new accommodations had to be added. Soon the property was studded with buildings offering additional guest quarters. Most were built by the Minetts, but the Manor House was once a resort unto itself, a small property known as Cheltonia House, which was owned by Charles Minett's niece, Louise and her husband William Fraling.

The hotel left the Minett family in 1958, but the pain was eased somewhat by the fact that the new owner, Ted Wright, was a good family friend. Wright had an engaging vision that would see Clevelands House undergo a new round of dramatic changes. During the entirety of the Minett era, the hotel had largely catered to a middle-aged crowd (indeed, families with young children were politely turned away). Wright's focus was on attracting younger guests. He introduced a wide-array of new recreational activities and attracted bands more in tune with young people. The focus was on creating a sense of vibrancy.

More changes came after 1969, when Bob Cornell and his wife, Fran, purchased Clevelands House. Bob began his career as a bellhop at the resort under the Minetts and worked his way up to becoming the resort's manager under Wright. Perhaps the most important change the Cornell's made was to shift the resort's focus from a singles resort to a family-friendly resort, as it remains today.

In the last few years, under new ownership, Clevelands House has undergone a series of ambitious

Clevelands House recently celebrated its 150th anniversary.

renovations aimed at restoring this iconic summer resort to its original splendor. Mission accomplished.

Despite the numerous changes, Clevelands House has seen over the years, the one thing that has remained the same is the atmosphere. Clevelands House was never intended to be luxurious, but rather homey, casual and welcoming. Fun, not formality, was the rule of the day. It remains that way today— a pleasing mix of modern and traditional, and an ideal vacation spot for families looking for leisure rather than elegance.

Note: Consider booking a room in Minett Lodge. You'll be sleeping in the same rooms as did Charles and Fanny and their children, as this was the home they built in 1870 to replace their original log cabin.

Clyffe House Cottage Resort

1010 Muskoka Road, Port Sydney
Web: www.clyffehouse.com
Email: reservations@clyffehouse.com
Phone: 705-704-9559

Clyffe House can trace its roots back to 1869 and has been in the same family since then.

In 1869, English immigrants, James and Fanny Jenner, homesteaded on the shores of Mary Lake. Like many settlers, the Jenner's found farming the soil rocky difficult, So shortly after the arrival of the railway in Huntsville in 1886, they began offering accommodations to hunters who came up in the autumn, demanding little more than a warm bed and a few home-cooked meals.

In 1905, their son, Robert, took over and converted the farmhouse into a resort called Clyffe House. Among the attractions that enticed guests was the unusually fine beach, almost a mile long, which

Mary Lake once had 25 resorts, but only Clyffe House remains.

gently descends into the lake for ideal swimming conditions.

The 1920s was the heyday of the resort. By then, the property had expanded to 400 acres with a dance hall, tennis courts, accommodations for more than 80 and a lively entertainment program. Among the famed guests were authors Robertson Davies and William McDonald.

A century later, Clyffe House Cottage Resort is the oldest resort in Muskoka still run continuously by the original founding family (now onto its fifth generation) and the only resort remaining of the 25 that once operated on Mary Lake. In most ways, it no longer resembles the resort of the exciting 1920s and 30s, when people danced the night away to big bands and dined in fancy dress, but the mere fact that Clyffe House endures is a testament to its enduring appeal and the passion of its owners.

Dee Bank Falls

Located at Muskoka Road 24 and North Shore Road.
The Falls are located 300 metres (.2 miles) north of the bridge.

Serene Dee Bank Falls was once home to a long-vanished hamlet and a towering grist mill.

Dee Bank Falls isn't the most dramatic waterfall in Muskoka, but picturesque and intimate, it is the remoteness of the falls that sets it apart. The water doesn't so much roar here as it murmurs. But even when the Dee River is at its highest, you can still walk on the rocks amidst the cascading waters, and oftentimes you'll have the falls completely to yourself.

The Dee River drains Three Mile Lake into Lake Rosseau. Just above the spanning bridge, the river slides down a steep incline, forming Dee Bank Falls. The setting is seemingly untouched, but in fact was once the heart of a thriving village named Dee Bank.

John Shannon built a grist mill here in 1868, the largest in Muskoka at the time, which served as the anchor for the hamlet. Grist mills were vital to settlers, and as a result, Dee Bank grew in prominence and prosperity. Soon there was also a school, sawmill, store, post office, an inn, church, cheese factory, tannery and blacksmith.

However, within a generation, the community had faded, and today it is gone completely. The only sound greeting those visiting Dee Bank is the sound of gurgling water. The sole remaining structure is the former schoolhouse, which dates back to the 1870s and was closed in 1965. One teacher, John Kaine, must have had an eye at a 90-degree angle in the small schoolhouse. "You couldn't get away with much," lamented Aubrey Bogart, a former pupil, "because he could see you fooling around even when his back was turned to write on the chalk board!"

DEERHURST RESORT

1235 Deerhurst Road
Web: www.deerhurstresort.com
Email: info@deerhurstresort.com
Phone: 1-800-461-4393

Charles Waterhouse built Deerhurst Resort in 1896. That summer he hosted two guests. Today, it is one of the largest and most prestigious resorts in Ontario.

Deerhurst is one of Muskoka's most enduring and prestigious resorts. The mere mention of the name conjures up images of warm service, elegant surroundings, captivating scenery and complete serenity.

In a way, Deerhurst was born of a dream. In 1896, high-born Englishman and recent immigrant Charles Waterhouse had a sudden vision: he would build a summer retreat along a stretch of prime waterfront on Peninsula Lake. Never mind that he had no experience running a resort, he was certain of success.

That's the kind of man Charles Waterhouse was: ambitious, tireless in pursuit of a goal and a dreamer.

Deerhurst was intended to be an inn of fine quality, offering comfortable accommodations to upper-class clientele, an island of casual refinement and British hospitality in the midst of the wilderness. Deerhurst stood out for being the first resort of any size operating in northern Muskoka.

Once the last guest of the season had left, Charles and Hylda packed up their belongings and returned to England for the winter. They remained until spring when they returned to prepare Deerhurst for another season of hospitality. Their first chore upon return was to jack up the building and even it out, since the building was without a foundation and would therefore shift throughout the freeze and thaw of winter. Some years the shifting was so bad the doors couldn't even be opened.

Regular guests during his period of management— the majority of whom were Americans—included such prominent and well-to-do families as the Grands of Grand and Toy fame; the Shirrifs, known for their jams and marmalades; the beer-brewing Seagrams; the Lambrechts; the Wadsworths, who included amongst them Presidents of Morgan-Stanley Bank; and others.

In 1925, 64-year-old Charles decided to retire from the hectic life of running a resort. It fell to his son Maurice to take over the reins of the hotel. A third generation, in the form of Bill Waterhouse, took over

The modern Lakeside Lodge units boast gorgeous views and sits on the site of Deerhurst's original lodge (pictured here).

in 1972, and it was he who was responsible for transforming Deerhurst from a rustic country inn into a modern, luxury resort with the finest amenities and a world-class reputation for refinement.

Waterhouse was most proud of the resort's unmatched live entertainment program. The resort hosted the Second City comedians, which included a teenaged Mike Myers, and had its own Vegas-style show. The show also held performances all over Ontario during the slow winter months, including at Roy Thomson Hall in Toronto and even the Grey Cup gala in Montreal. The resort became known as the "Vegas of the North." Also among the hundreds of performers who passed through Deerhurst was a very young, very ambitious Shania Twain.

By 1989, Bill Waterhouse no longer found any challenge in Deerhurst. His work had been done, his vision accomplished: Deerhurst was now fully modernized and one of the elite resorts in Ontario. When an attractive offer to sell was presented to him, Bill didn't hesitate for long.

Although it would never be the same without the Waterhouse family, Deerhurst endured. What's more, it continued to evolve and define itself so that today, 20 years later, Deerhurst is undoubtedly one of Canada's most impressive resort properties. Set in 800 acres of wilderness, Deerhurst allows visitors to appreciate the outdoors while still enjoying the lap of luxury, blending a year-round natural playground setting with the height in guest comforts and engaging service. For those who want an active stay, there are all sorts of exciting activities to choose from, including golf (Deerhurst Highlands, one of two 18-hole courses on the property, was named one of ScoreGolf's top public courses in Canada), boating and horseback riding in the summer and dog-sledding and cross-country skiing in the winter. People who are looking for relaxation can unwind at the full-service spa, sink into a bubbling hot-tub or cuddle up to the inviting warmth of a fireplace.

Simply put, even a few nights at Deerhurst is pure indulgence—the kind not easily forgotten.

Note: Perched on the site of Deerhurst's original lodge (built in 1896) is the magnificent new Lakeside Lodge, offering one, two and three bedroom condos with cottage-inspired décor.

Dorset Heritage Museum

1040 Main Street, Dorset
Admission
Web: www.dorsetheritagemuseum.ca
Phone: 705-766-0323
Email: dhm@muskoka.com

Dorset was founded by Zac Cole, a veteran of the American Civil War. The Dorset Heritage Museum preserves the community's rich history.

The pioneer spirit is at home in Dorset. For almost 20 years, the Dorset Heritage Museum has showcased artifacts recalling the early history of this community.

Dorset was originally called Cedar Narrows for the cedar trees that proliferated here. Zac Cole, the first settler, changed the name to Colebridge. He built the community's first inn, the Colebridge Hotel (located where Robinson's General Store stands today), catering equally to lumbermen and weary travellers making their way along the rutted roads.

Others soon joined the Coles, and by the early 1880s a village had taken root. Cole applied for a post office in 1883 and found there was already a postal district called Colebridge, so chose the name Dorset instead.

One winter night in 1885, Cole died after tripping and striking his head on the stove. As per his request, he was buried in a coffin of tamarack (a wood that snaps loudly in the fire) so that when it burned in hell everyone would know he was there.

The community Cole had helped found was largely sustained by logging. Angus Mackay built a sawmill in town in 1894 and donated lumber for the construction of Knox United Church. His grandson, Norm, helped found the Dorset Heritage Museum in 2001.

The museum's exhibits focus on early pioneer life, the stories of colourful settlers like Cole and logging practices as would have been used by Angus MacKay and others of his ilk.

Tip: Visit on Heritage Day, held annually on the July 1st long weekend. Activities include steam-powered farm equipment on display, re-enactors reliving Muskoka's military past, a marketplace and demonstrations of pioneer handicrafts.

Dorset Scenic Tower

1191 Dorset Scenic Tower Road
Web: www. Algonquinhighlands.ca
Email: tower@algonquinhighlands.ca
Phone: 705-766-1032

The observation deck of the tower in Dorset is 142 metres above lake level and provides a panoramic view of more than 800 square kilometres.

Muskoka has many locations that offer stunning vistas of fall forests, transformed into a painter's palette of vivid colours, but none is as spectacular as that from atop the scenic tower in Dorset.

In the 1920s—for the first time really—the Ontario government began to pay attention to the protection of its forests. In 1922, Ontario Lands and Forests (the predecessor of MNR) built a fire station in Dorset, where the Dorset Heritage Museum is located today. A fire tower atop the adjacent hill, known locally as "The Mountain," was completed in 1928. There were no stairs to the tower's observation deck; the only way up was an iron ladder with guide rings.

The fire tower remained in service until 1961, by which time it was considered obsolete and replaced by aerial surveillance. The aging tower was dismantled, and its parts were sent to Algonquin Park for exhibit.

People soon realized that the scenic view previously enjoyed only by tower-men represented a potential tourist draw, and so a replacement, slightly taller (30m/100ft) tower was built in 1967, thankfully, with stairs instead of a ladder. From its observation deck some 142 metres (465 feet) above lake level, you're awarded a panoramic view encompassing 803 square kilometres (310 square miles). On a clear autumn day, the view is enthralling. Don't like heights? You can remain safely on the ground and still enjoy a pleasant view thanks to the elevation of The Mountain.

The site also includes picnic tables, a gift shop and 2.5 kilometres (1.5 miles) of hiking trails.

Dunn's Pavilion (Kee to Bala)

1012 Bala Falls Road, Bala
Admission by Event
Web: www.thekee.com
Phone: 705-762-3134

Dunn's Pavilion played host to the biggest names of the Big Band era, including Duke Ellington, Guy Lombardo and the Dorsey Brothers.

It was known as "The Place Where All the World Dances." The brightest names of the Big Band era played here for night crowds of as many as 1500 exultant young people, placing the spotlight firmly on the village of Bala and Bala on the tourist map. This Muskoka landmark was Dunn's Pavilion.

In 1929, Toronto pharmacist Gerry Dunn purchased Walter Langdon's Dance Hall business in Bala. Within a decade the popularity of the dance hall demanded expansion, so in 1942, Dunn tore down the old building and raised in its place a much larger venue.

Dunn's Pavilion was a magical place. The building's exterior was decorated with flower boxes and palm trees. Inside, the bandstand resembled the front of a quaint cottage. On warm nights, dancers cooled off on the outdoor balcony overlooking Bala Bay. Dunn enforced a strict dress code: ladies wore dresses or evening gowns, while men donned jackets and ties.

Dunn's Pavilion attracted the biggest musical names of the age to Bala, among them Louis Armstrong, Guy Lombardo, Woody Herman, Duke Ellington, Les Brown and his Band of Renown, Count Basie, Glen Miller and the Dorsey Brothers. For 10 years, starting in 1943, Mart Kenny and his band, Live Show, broadcast live from Dunn's on Sundays at 7:00 PM. Admission was $5, but many enjoyed free concerts by parking their boats out on the water.

The building is still there (though faded from its heyday) and continues to host concerts under the name The Kee to Bala.

Note: Musquash Road is Bala's original main street. It became a quiet side street when the current route of Highway 169 through town opened in 1964.

DYER MEMORIAL NATURE RESERVE

Dyer Road (off Williamsport Road), Huntsville
No Admission
Web: www.muskokaconservancy.org
Email: info@muskokaconservancy.org
Phone: 705-645-7393

The little-known Dyer Memorial is a love letter from a grieving husband to his departed wife.

Nature-lovers and history buffs alike will find something to enjoy in the far northern reaches of Muskoka. Hidden amidst the all-encompassing forests and appearing out of the trees as if by magic is a lush, gardenlike grove anchored by a towering stone monument. This is the Dyer Memorial.

In 1916, Clifton Dyer and his wife, Betsy, honeymooned in Algonquin Park. They returned to the region to celebrate their 20th wedding anniversary, during which they canoed the Big East River. The couple fell deeply in love with the rugged beauty and soul-soothing tranquility of the wilderness along the Big East. In 1940 they decided to build a cottage on the bank of the river, the very spot they camped four years earlier.

The Dyer's returned to their wilderness idyll every year until Betsy's death in 1956. Devastated by the loss, Clifton was determined to memorialize Betsy in some way, and the result is truly moving.

On the highest point of the property, overlooking the Big East River, Clifton erected a 12-metre (40-foot) stone cairn. On top, he placed a copper urn holding Betsy's ashes, offering her an eternal view of the landscape she cherished. Clifton inscribed the stone with the words: "An affectionate, loyal and understanding wife is life's greatest gift."

Surrounding the cairn is a 390-square-metre (4290-square-foot) flagstone terrace and beyond that a 10-acre (4-hectare) park with rolling lawns, a pond and botanical gardens. Following his death in 1959, Clifton's ashes were placed in an urn next to his wife's.

Falkenburg and St. George's Anglican Church

Muskoka Road 4, just north of Bracebridge (church) and Moore Road (ghost town)

In its heyday, the ghost town of Falkenburg was sustained by the Moore sawmill.

As you drive north on Muskoka Road 4 from Bracebridge, watch for St. George's Anglican Church, a tangible reminder of one of the oldest ghost towns in Muskoka.

At one time, Falkenburg was bigger and more prosperous than Bracebridge, thanks to its strategic location at the crossroads of two colonization roads— the Parry Sound Colonization Road and the Muskoka Colonization Road. It boasted a pair of hotels, an Orange Lodge, school, store, blacksmith shop, Matthias Moore's sawmill and St. George's Anglican Church.

Headstones in the Falkenburg cemetery bear witness to the harshness of life in early Muskoka. Jane Samway, Matthias Moore's daughter-in-law, died in childbirth at age 24. Her husband, Frank, left for Toronto, leaving Matthias to raise his three grandchildren.

Falkenburg's fate was sealed when the railway came through in 1866, bypassing Falkenburg. The entire village, church included, moved a few kilometres south alongside the newly-laid railway tracks (not far beyond these railway tracks is an unpaved trail that veers off to the north-east; this was the original Muskoka Road leading to Falkenburg). The Moore family continued in the lumbering trade, but also opened a general store.

Not much remains of Falkenburg beyond the Moore's original home, the cemetery and the old Muskoka Road that fades into bush. Try to imagine a time when the land here was cleared of trees and replaced by fields of crops.

Note: The fully restored Moore store sits on the grounds of Muskoka Heritage Place in Huntsville where it is known as the Hays General Store, named after its original owners.

Fenian Fort

Behind the RE/MAX Hallmark Realty Ltd. Building, 114 Medora St., Port Carling
No Admission

Port Carling's stone fort was built to defend against the threat of a Fenian invasion.

The stone walls at Fenian Fort are low but intimidating, evoking an image of sturdy defiance. The squat fortress looks all the larger for its position atop a bluff above Port Carling, looming over the village and its locks. Trees, shrubs and clumps of tough-looking weeds grow inside the walls—the sign of human abandonment—and yet the defenses look surprisingly robust, ready to defend the village against threats, though one hasn't existed for one and a half centuries.

It is here, above Port Carling and behind a forested shroud, that one of Muskoka's most mysterious structures lies.

In 1868, several hundred members of the radical Irish Nationalist group known as the Fenian Botherhood gathered arms and crossed over to Canada from Buffalo. Their goal was to hold the British Dominion hostage: Britain must free Ireland or Canada would suffer further depravations and perhaps even a full invasion. Although the invaders were few in number, they were all hardened by the battles of the American Civil War and steeled by the patriotic resolve to free Ireland from British control. They had little trouble defeating an ill-prepared force of Canadian defenders at Fort Erie and Ridgeway before retreating, victorious, back across the border. The intent of the raid was to sow terror in Canada, and they succeeded.

To the people of Ontario in the late 1860s, the Fenian threat was as frightening as the Red Scare of the 1950s or the fear that gripped America after 9/11. There were hundreds of thousands of Irish in the United States, many of them combat veterans of the Civil War. People in Ontario began to see Fenian boogeymen under every bed and in every shadow. The Fenian raid of 1868—and others of its kind—forced Canadians everywhere to realize just how vulnerable they were to such attacks. One of those people was Port Carling resident Robert Hardcastle Johnston.

Robert Hardcastle Johnston, a bewhiskered and eccentric gentleman, was one of the founders of Port Carling. Johnston was a prominent man among the young community, becoming its first postmaster in 1868. That same year, the Fenians raided into Canada. Johnston took note. He had petitioned long and hard to have the provincial government build locks in Port Carling and worried that the Fenians might sabotage this economically important infrastructure.

To protect his beloved locks, Johnston built an imposing stone-walled fortification on the crest of a high hill where defenders could see down the Indian River and onto Steamship Bay. In an era when Port Carling was denuded of trees by lumbermen, any approaching boat would be seen from this commanding position. It would also serve as a strongpoint to which citizens could retreat in time of danger and resist invaders. When finished, the stronghold looked like something like a Bronze Age hill fort.

Luckily, the protective walls were never required as no Irish raiders ever came near Muskoka. The Fenian raids ended in 1871 and with it the paranoia that paralyzed Ontario lifted. The fort was now without purpose.

William Hanna, community leader and store-keeper, later built a water tower inside the fortifications to provide nearby residents with water under the name of Port Carling Water Supply Company.

Johnston's former fort served this function until 1947, when the municipal council took responsibility for providing water to the entire community. After this, the fort sat empty, a mysterious stone shell whose purpose most in town had long-since forgotten.

The low walls of the fort still remain atop that hill, standing silent sentinel over Port Carling. Though hidden by dense foliage for much of the year, the eerie ruins are visible behind the Re/Max Hallmark Realty building after the leaves drop in the autumn.

GERMANIA

6 kilometres (3.7 miles) south of Muskoka Road 118 on
Germania Road

As the name implies, the ghost town of Germania was founded
predominantly by German settlers. The church in which they
worshipped still stands.

Germania was a farming hamlet that—as the
name implies—was settled by people of Germanic
origin with dreams of transforming the forest into
fields of swaying wheat. For a time they even
succeeded, but Germania faded in the 20th century.
Today, you'd hardly know a village that once boasted
a sawmill, general store, blacksmith shop and a number of prosperous farms once stood huddled around
these corners.

However, a number of atmospheric remnants remain, reminding us of the community's history.

Sadly the school, built in 1888 and where lessons were originally taught in German, has recently collapsed and is now a jumble of rotting boards. The Gilbert Lutheran Church, however, still stands and is virtually unaltered from the day it opened in 1876. It is still heated by an old wood stove; the pews are original, and the mouse-proof pump organ donated to the congregation in 1921 remains. The original land grant is proudly mounted on the wall. Across the street is the Gilbert homestead, once one of the most prosperous farms in Germania, complete with a fine dairy herd, orchard and many hectares of oats and beans.

A more tragic reminder of the village's past hides in the southwest corner of the graveyard in a secluded and overgrown area. A small gravestone, sinking into the ground, belongs to Katherine Dietz, who died in 1903, aged 29. Unwed and yet heavy with child, Katherine felt she had brought shame upon her family. In desperation, she waded into Weismuller Lake, her dress and petticoat, wool coat and leather shoes serving as an anchor. Because she had committed the double sin of suicide and unwed pregnancy, Katherine was buried away from family and friends, as alone in death as she must have felt in those final despondent days.

Glen Orchard

Highway 169, north of Bala

The 1890 Glen Orchard schoolhouse is a designated heritage structure.

The hamlet of Glen Orchard had a notably inauspicious beginning.

Snow fell heavily that November day in 1868, settling in deep drifts and driving on a biting wind into the faces of John and Susan (Henshaw) Nixon. John pulled up the collar of his coat as he urged the struggling ox forward, while Susan slunk further under the blanket wrapped tightly around her.

While crossing a bridge, the snow-blinded ox slipped and tumbled into the bog below. The husband-and-wife settlers spent several miserable hours freeing the animal from the mire. Finally, they arrived at their Ada Lake lot where they would set down roots.

Despite this harrowing start, Susan sent glowing reports of the region to her family, and soon several relatives joined them to settle along the shores of what became known as Henshaw Lake.

Family friend Nathaniel Orchard also came, building a home on the site of the current Glen Orchard store and, in 1877, becoming postmaster. Since his home was located in a glen between Ada Lake and Butterfly Lake, he chose to call it Glen Orchard.

While Glen Orchard never reached the heights envisioned by Susan Nixon when she encouraged others to join her and her husband 150 years ago, the community endures.

A tangible reminder of the hamlet's early days can be found along White's Road. Here, huddled within the Glen Orchard Cemetery, stands the circa-1890 schoolhouse. Within its walls are the hopes of the area's settlers for a prosperous future. In recognition of its history, the Township of Muskoka Lakes designated the Glen Orchard Schoolhouse as a heritage property under the Ontario Heritage Act.

GRAVENHURST GATEWAY ARCH

Muskoka Road just off Highway 11, Gravenhurst

There have been five arches welcoming people to Gravenhurst, dating to 1874.

Gravenhurst bills itself as the Gateway to Muskoka. There's some literal truth to this—it is, indeed, the first town one arrives at when driving north along Highway 11, and in times past when steamship was the primary mode of transportation, virtually everyone coming to or from Muskoka would have transited the town. It is therefore appropriate that there would be a physical gateway marking the entrance to Gravenhurst.

The current gateway—a popular spot for tourists to snap photos—is just the latest in a series of gateways erected in Gravenhurst over the years.

The first gate was an arch of pine boughs to welcome Lord Dufferin, the Governor General of Canada (1872–78), when he passed through with his wife in 1874.

In 1885, the town again draped itself in pine boughs to honour the arrival of yet another Governor General, the Fifth Marquis of Landsdowne, when he and his wife made a brief tour of Muskoka. The Mickle-Dyment and Son Company, which ran a massive sawmill in Gravenhurst, raised an even more impressive arch at the town wharf to commemorate Landsdowne's visit. This elaborate arch, designed to reflect the lumber industry, was a wooden structure decorated with circular saws, crosscut saws, axes, drive belts, chains, snowshoes, pike poles and a rowboat (called a pointer; a type used in log drives).

Later archways were built by the town itself to promote Gravenhurst among tourists as the springboard for vacations and adventure in Muskoka. The present attractive gateway was erected in 2009 and is a replica of an earlier one, built in 1925.

Gravenhurst Opera House

95 Muskoka Road South, Gravenhurst
Admission by performance
Web: www.gravenhurst.ca/en/explore-and-play/
opera-house.aspx
Phone: 705-687-5550

The Gravenhurst Opera House is the birthplace of summer theatre in Ontario.

The Gravenhurst Opera House is a Muskoka landmark. One of the finest examples of Victorian theatre construction north of Toronto and the undisputed birthplace of Canadian summer theatre, it has seen countless dramas over the century since its construction, playing out both on and off stage.

Located along a busy thoroughfare in the heart of Gravenhurst, the Opera House remains safely cocooned in the Victorian-era. The building is so authentic that Murdoch Mysteries—the mystery series starring Yannick Bisson—has filmed here several times. The Opera House, it seems, was born for the spotlight.

Gravenhurst's original town hall was razed in a fire that swept the town in July 1897 and reduced much of the community to ash and smoke-blackened rubble. Work started on a replacement in early 1900 under the expert eye of two of the region's most accomplished builders: Frank Smith Hurlbut, who built Minnewaska Resort and Wigwassan Lodge on Lake Rosseau's Tobin Island, and stonemason William McKay, who had helped build the Orillia Opera House in 1894.

The building that emerged in March 1901 was uncommonly grand for what was still a small, northern community. Constructed solely of brick with extensive municipal offices on the first floor, a cavernous theatre above and topped with an impressive tower that naturally carried observing eyes skyward, the combined town hall and theatre was something worthy of community pride.

For the first three decades, the stage was largely occupied by local productions or vaudeville acts. A new form of entertainment emerged in 1934 when John Holden arrived in Gravenhurst with his company, The Good Companions, to stage professional summer theatre—the first in Canada. The Graven-hurst Opera House is known today as the birthplace of Canadian summer theatre as a result.

Some of Canada's greatest talents have performed on the Opera House's stage. Donald Sutherland, star of countless Hollywood films, made his acting debut here. Sutherland had first been at the Opera House in 1955, "paying his dues" as a stage carpenter, but returned as a full-fledged actor the following two summers. Bond-girl Honor Blackman performed here in 1952, as did Doc Williams, the country super-star of his era, in 1956. Other names include Gordon Lightfoot, Michael Burgess, Graham Green, Megan Follows and Helen Shaver, who have all had their names prominently displayed on the billboards at various times. In the realm of what might have been, starlet and Blonde Bombshell Jane Mansfield had been scheduled to perform at the Opera House in 1957, but the show was cancelled last minute.

Performers love the theatre's distinctive wooden "ship's hull" ceiling, which many believe—celebrated Canadian singer Diana Krall among them—help to make the chamber "acoustically perfect."

By the 1990s, however, such heady days were well in the past. The aging building was in dire need of renovations, resulting in an expensive restoration. The famed acoustical excellence of the old Opera House and its visual charm survived, but thanks to the renovations, the comfortable old building was now an elegant heritage showcase for both

Gravenhurst and Muskoka. One foot remained comfortably in the early 20th century, while the other stepped toward the new century.

Throughout the years, despite the changes in the community, the evolution of entertainment and all the dramas, one thing has remained consistent: the Opera House was, and remains today, at the heart of Gravenhurst.

The Opera House continues to host summer theatre but is also a year-round facility with an ambitious line-up of comedy, music and dramatic performances. It is also the home of the Muskoka Independent Film Festival and participates in the annual Sawdust City Music Festival, a multi-venue event celebrating Canadian music.

One of only four Victorian period theatres still operating in Ontario, the Gravenhurst Opera House remains as vibrant as when the curtains were first raised in 1901. The administrative offices and magistrate courts are gone, but the opera house continues to host all manners of live entertainment. Though at times it looked as if the curtains might fall on the Gravenhurst Opera House, the passionate community has made sure that there has always been a new act.

Note: The Opera House is fronted by the Opera House Square, which includes the community cenotaph.

GRIFFIN PUB AND CHANCERY LANE

9 Chancery Lane (off Manitoba Street), Bracebridge
Web: www.thegriffinpub.ca
Email: events@thegriffinpub.ca
Phone: 705-646-0438

Two criminals were hung atop atmospheric Chancery Lane, which today is home to an art gallery and a gastropub.

Chancery Lane feels like something out of the Old World—a characterful, cobble-stoned alley-way framed by an attractive iron gate that passes between business blocks in downtown Bracebridge. Named after a street in London where the main courts and lawyers were located, the lane was aptly named when it was built in 1883 to allow for easy access to the courthouse and Town Hall that were located atop the laneway.

Lawyers still ascend Chancery Lane today on their way to the current Muskoka District Courthouse, built in 1990. Many take lunch in a bar atop the lane: Griffin Pub, an atmospheric establishment that blends good food, great company, Ontario's best craft beers and friendly hospitality into one memorable package. But more than all that, the building housing the Griffin Pub is rich in history. For most of its history, the building was—fittingly, considering its clientele—the office of lawyer Russell Maxwell Best.

R.M. Best, born in Toronto, headed north to Bracebridge in 1920. Recently returned from World War One, where he served as an artillery officer, the highly educated 26-year-old was in search of new opportunities and a community where he could leave his mark. He purchased the law firm of the late George Mahaffy and occupied a wooden building at the northwest corner of Chancery Lane. This aged square-frame structure, which dated to the late 19th century and was originally a Chinese laundry, was growing weary by the time Best took over. The ambitious lawyer endured the drafty walls until he could get his practice on solid footing. By the early 1930s, having been named King's Counsel, Best was prospering and looking toward erecting a new building that was a better reflection of his standing in the community. With that in mind, Best had the old

Historic Bracebridge Courthouse

building taken down around 1933 and a handsome two-story brick building raised in its place. Law offices were located on the main floor with an apartment for his associates located above.

After an illustrious career spanning more than 60 years, Best retired in 1980. He wasn't fated to enjoy a long retirement, however, dying a mere year later in 1981.

After standing empty for several years, Best's former law office became the Griffin Pub in 1998, catering largely to the lawyers working at the nearby courthouse. During renovations, the brick walls and heavy steel door of a closet-sized safe—which would have been used by Best to secure documents, bond money and the like—were uncovered. The safe has been incorporated into the pub by being transformed into a washroom.

Most of those enjoying the pub's intimate patio have no idea they are dining within a stone's throw of the former jail and the unmarked grave of one of only two men ever hung in Muskoka.

George Cyr was impoverished and often barely able to put food on the table for his family. Thanks to tireless toil, his neighbors, Andrew and Lena Solave, were slightly better off, and Cyr often looked upon them in jealousy. When he got wind that the Solaves' son had sent them a large sum of money, Cyr saw an opportunity. On a frigid December day in 1921, Cyr arriving at the Solave farm in a hail of bullets, gunned down Lena and Andrew, along with another neighbour, George Wethers, who happened to be at their home. Lena and Wethers died, while Andrew managed to stumble into the woods and to safety.

George Cyr was hanged for his crime and his body buried in an unmarked grave atop Chancery Lane, likely only metres from the Griffin Pub.

Gristmill Park

Highway 117 in Baysville, east side of the Muskoka River

Pulford House welcomed guests to Baysville for half a century, starting in 1906. Its grounds are now a waterside park.

The town of Baysville was a late comer to the resort business. Alexander Judson Henderson, brother-in-law of Baysville founder, William H. Brown, opened the area's first resort in 1906.

The resort Henderson built was an attractive two-storey structure with more than a dozen guestrooms, a dancefloor upstairs and a winch that lifted heavy steamer trunks from wagons (and later automobiles) parked outside directly to the upper rooms. He named it Pulford House in honor of his only child, Pulford Henderson.

The aging A.J. Henderson sold the resort in 1922. John James and Elizabeth Robertson were the new owners, and so Pulford House became the Robertson Inn. A professional tennis player from Indiana, who vacationed in the area, gave lessons for the guests.

In 1946, the resort burned to the ground. With its demise, most of the expansive grounds were sold to the Department of Highways, who needed the land to build a new bridge, but a portion was made into an attractive riverside park known as Gristmill Park.

Grindstones from the town's gristmill were incorporated into a memorial honouring Baysville's World War veterans (hence the park's name). Bill Gammage built the mill on the opposite side of the river in 1877. A man of many disciplines, he also operated a store where farmers could exchange their grain for goods.

The park's pretty waterline—the feature which inspired A.J. Henderson to build a resort here a century ago—offers a pleasant stroll, but sadly of Henderson's dream, nothing remains except for fading memories in the minds of a few aging townsfolk.

HATCHERY PARK AND FALLS

Fish Hatchery Road, Utterson (the park is on the left, about
one kilometre/.6 miles down the road)
Admission free

One of Muskoka's secret gems, a tranquil waterfall, is found in
the woods at Hatchery Park.

Hatchery Falls, named for the Ministry of Natural
Resources fish hatchery that operated just upstream
of the falls for decades, is one of the best-kept secrets
in Muskoka. Few people know this 8-metre (26-foot)
tall waterfall even exists. Now the secret is out.

A century ago, dozens of sawmills operating across
the region fouled the lakes and streams with sawdust, destroying spawning grounds for fish species.
Combined with years of heavy recreational fishing
by tourists and sustenance fishing by settlers, this

threatened to destroy stocks of important fish in numerous lakes and unhinge the delicate ecological balance. In response to the crisis, the Ontario Department of Game and Fisheries developed the Skeleton Lake Fish Culture Station in 1937 (perhaps better known as the Skeleton Lake Fish Hatchery). The station, set on 18 acres of land that, in an almost ironic twist, had once been the site of a thriving saw-mill, is adjacent to Skeleton Lake which empties into the Skeleton River.

The hatchery was part of a concerted effort to repair half a century of damage, breeding small mouth bass, walleye, lake trout and muskellunge to restock the lakes. The situation was so dire that annual production throughout the 1940s and '50s averaged 300,000 speckled trout, 350,000 pickerel and 100,000 small mouth bass.

The effort to restock our lakes worked better than most would have dreamed possible. In fact, the Hatchery worked so well that it put itself out of business. In 1992, the Ministry of Natural Resources closed the facility.

When he heard there was talk of selling and developing the land, Aubrey Goltz, who served as Director of the Township of Muskoka Lakes Rate Payers' Association, knew he had to act to preserve public access to one of Muskoka's few remaining untouched waterfalls. Together with the eager assistance of the local residents and students of nearby Watt Public School, Goltz managed to convince the township to

Hatchery Falls is nestled in a tranquil oasis in the woods.

purchase the land and develop a park. Tragically, Goltz passed away before work was completed and never got to see the park as he had so often envisioned it. Undoubtedly, he'd have been thrilled and likely touched by the bronze plaque mounted on a large rock in the center of the park, memorializing him and his efforts.

Hatchery Park allows you to immerse yourself in the natural world. A one-kilometre (.6-mile) trail leads through fields and light woods on the former Hatchery grounds, along the riverbank and past the overgrown fish culture ponds. You can read the various interpretive signs (gifts of the Muskoka Heritage Foundation) which describe points of interest along the pathways and offer information on the various plants and wildlife that thrive in this natural oasis. You might learn, for example, that muskrat and deer feed upon the sweet gale that grows along the river's shoreline, and that Nuttall's Pond Weed, the only vegetation growing on the sandy bed of the otherwise crystal-clear waterway, is a major source of food for ducks. These informative plaques make the park more than just a place of recreation, but also of environmental education.

Hatchery Park is interesting in its own right, but there's something even more spectacular to see, hiding within the forest. You'll notice a trail that disappears into the woods, following the course of the river. Venture along it. Soon, the faint sound of rushing water tells you that you're headed toward a waterfall. The trail is rough, strewn with rocks and tree roots, but the end result is well worth any scrambling you have to do along the 15-minute hike.

The falls can only be described as an unspoiled treasure. It tumbles over a steep cascade into a plunge pool surrounded by high, rocky hills. Untouched by humanity, without bridges or other structures to intrude upon the scene, and with the sound of the raging water silencing everything else in the area, it's a magical and unexpected discovery.

High Falls

Muskoka Road 117, off Highway 11. The entrance to the park is immediately west of the Highway on the right.
No Admission

High Falls. The only true waterfall in Muskoka

The most spectacular waterfall in Muskoka is almost certainly High Falls. Even at the height of summer the sound of its thundering water is almost deafening. The only falls in Muskoka that can truly be called a falls, the water drops over a sheer cliff in a vertical curtain of raging water, just like Niagara. The other waterfalls in Muskoka, by contrast, are more properly classified as "cascades," since they descend down a rock face in a series of steps without losing contact with the bedrock.

High Falls stands an imposing 20 metres (65 feet) in height, and, at one point, travel promoters eager to lure people to Muskoka labeled it the "Niagara of the North." It is a bit of an exaggeration, but it accurately reflects High Falls' stature as the most prominent waterfall anywhere in Cottage Country. In fact, you have to travel as far north as Wawa to find a waterfall larger.

Perhaps unsurprisingly, the Town of Bracebridge decided to harness the substantial power of High Falls in 1948. Thankfully, the generating station is hidden from the view of visitors to High Falls Park on the south side of the river. Here, looking between the cedars, all you see is water, mist, and the blue expanse of sky.

Note: Watch for a cairn dedicated to Aubrey White, the man known as "The Father of Forest Protection in Ontario." As assistant commissioner of Crown Lands, the former lumberman created the first system of fire ranging in the province in 1885.

Hilltop Interiors

1150 Highway 141, Rosseau
Web: www.hilltopinteriors.com
Email: design@hilltopinteriors.com
Phone: 705-732-4040

Located in the heart of the charming village of Rosseau, Hilltop Interiors offers tasteful décor and home furnishings.

Shoppers entering Hilltop Interiors will find no shortage of ideas for decorating their home or cottage, but behind the stylish décor and furniture is a rich history dating back to the village's earliest years.

Rosseau wasn't a village—hardly even a collection of homes scratched out of the forest—when English-man Samuel Greer arrived in 1872. One year later, he erected a store, the first commercial business in Rosseau, on the site that is occupied today by Hilltop Interiors.

Greer didn't last too long, and neither did the next sequence of owners, which included William Ashdown, an industrious gentleman who ran a store and hotel in the nearby village of Ashdown Corners (a community now long gone); George Raymond, who had a bakery and bar in the building alongside the store; and George Brown, who had succeeded Ashdown as Ashdown Corner's storekeeper. Later, Brown took over possession of the Rosseau store and opened the community's first public library on the premises—even if the library was little more than a glass case containing a handful of books.

In 1922, Brown decided to move his business to the store across the street (the modern day Rosseau General Store) and sold his first mercantile to George Albert Atkinson. Atkinson was an interesting and enterprising character. Under his ownership, the main part of the building remained a store, a corner of which was given over to a post office and express service. He also operated a stage business out of the shop. Finally, he served as village undertaker; bodies were prepared for burial in a room, stacked high with coffins, off of the retail space. A large barn behind the store housed Atkinson's horses, stage coach and the grim hearse.

Tragically, the store burned down on November 1, 1925, depriving us of what would have been a truly

Hilltop Interiors. Dating to 1925, the building housing Hilltop Interiors was at various times a store, an undertaker's shop and a tearoom.

special historic building. Thankfully, perhaps with an eye towards posterity, Atkinson rebuilt the new store as a virtual duplicate of the original. The only significant difference was the lack of a verandah on the replacement.

Atkinson ran the store until his death in 1945. The building was sold to Victor and Isabelle Whight, who transformed it into a tea room serving light lunches and desserts. Tourists flocking to the region soon began stopping at Hilltop Tea Room; for the first time, the building was on the map for out-of-towners.

The Whight's daughter, Mae, and her husband, Ellis Gates, played an increasing role in running the establishment in the late 1940s. They brought with them youthful energy and a different vision.

A few years later, the Whight's sold out. A carousel of owners came and went over the decades, and the building at various times served as a gift shop, an antique store and a local handicrafts shop.

The building was reinvigorated in December 2000 when interior decorator Lena Patten and her husband Randy purchased the aging building with an eye toward making it both a home décor store and a base for her interior decorating business. In honor of the tearoom of yesteryear, they named it Hilltop Interiors. Lena is proud to have maintained much of the original building during renovations, and equally proud that she and her family—including their two then-young boys—did the work themselves.

Hilltop Interiors is a must-visit as much for its historic significance as for its tasteful décor and inspiring design ideas.

Tip: Lena Patten loves Christmas—truly, madly loves it—so visit during the holiday season for festive flourishes for your home. Aim for Hilltop Interiors' annual Christmas open house.

Indian Landing

South Mary Lake Road, south end of Port Sydney
No Admission

Indian Landing is one of the most photographed spots in Muskoka.

One of the most photographed autumn spots in Muskoka, Indian Landing evokes understated beauty.

The gravel bar on the southwest side of the bridge in Port Sydney has come to be known as Indian Landing. For centuries, the Muskoka River had served as a highway for Indigenous people. They would traverse its length in canoes and arrive each spring as they headed north to summer hunting grounds and again in the fall as they headed south to winter quarters. While passing through what is today Port Sydney, they would come across a small waterfall and a set of dangerous rapids, which they would sensibly portage around.

Generations of people have assumed the portage was on the west bank, and thus the name Indian Landing. In actuality, however, the First Nation portage was on the river's east bank of the river.

Port Sydney's first settler, John McAlpine, who arrived in 1868, ignored centuries of tradition when travelling along the river. Instead of portaging around the rapids, he would shoot them in a dug-out canoe called the Man-Killer. To the surprise of most neighbours, he survived his recklessness.

The frothing and raging rapids that bedeviled these early travellers are long gone. The turbulent water represented an obstacle for lumbermen shepherding logs down the river and bulldozers and dams were used to eliminate them. Still, the site remains serenely beautiful, a spot where waters gently ripple and reflect the colours of trees that hang over the banks.

Inn at the Falls

8 Mahaffy Ct., Bracebridge
Web: www.innatthefalls.ca
Email: reservations@innatthefalls.ca
Phone: 705-645-2245

Famed in equal measure for history and haunts, Inn at the Falls has been lovingly renovated and welcomes guests with a delightful meal and comfortable overnight accommodations.

Everything about the newly revitalized Inn at the Falls impresses. Recent renovations and redesign to this Bracebridge landmark have been done with a warmth and attention to detail, resulting in an inviting space that feels elegant and appealing. Best of all, ownership has gone to great lengths to balance the new with the old. After all, the inn's long and colorful history is a big part of its appeal.

Standing only a block from Bracebridge's main street and its trademark waterfall, the historic two-storey hotel has been at the heart of the community for almost 150 years. Inn at the Falls was originally built in 1876 as the home of lawyer John Adair. It was, at the time, the grandest house in Bracebridge, a town that was growing rapidly but was still rough around the edges. A year later, Adair sold the magnificent manor to William C. Mahaffy, an ambitious 29-year-old man preparing to open his own law practice there.

In the years that followed, Mahaffy would leave his stamp both on the building and upon the young town. In 1888, he was appointed the first District Court Judge of Muskoka and Parry Sound, becoming the youngest District Court Judge in Canada. He was also a land surveyor and, perhaps unsurprisingly, a landholder—his property extended to Main Street and as far north as Chancellery Lane. While he was growing wealthy, Mahaffy was also rising within the ranks of influential fraternities such as the Loyal Orange Lodge (it's even rumored meetings of these organizations were held in the basement of Inn at the Falls). Arguably the most prominent man about town, Mahaffy's home was the centre of social, political and economic life in Bracebridge for years.

By 1912, however, William Mahaffy was wilting under the debilitating effects of a disease, likely cancer. He went to England for treatment but never returned, dying there on June 14 of that year at the age of 64. A few years after the judge's death, Mahaffy's widow sold the Dominion Street home and for the next several decades it passed from hand to hand, no owner staying very long.

A new chapter began in 1943 when Ernie and Marion Allchin purchased the house, made extensive renovations and opened it as the Holiday House Hotel. Accommodating up to 35 guests, it welcomed summer guests from all over the world and proved an instant success.

The next eight decades saw many changes, some purposeful, some by sudden necessity. On October 20, 1955, fire broke out on the top floor of the hotel and spread rapidly. Thanks to the quick action of the local fire department, the building was saved, but damage was extensive and required a complete rebuild of the upper levels. In 1962, an authentic British-style pub was built in the basement where stables and a furnace room were once located. Then, in 1988, new owners Bill and Sylvia Richardson unveiled a new name: Inn at the Falls, reflecting its position atop a bluff overlook-ing Bracebridge's thundering waterfall. More accom-modations were added when an additional building, The Mews, was built with large, contemporary rooms offering private balconies overlooking the picturesque Bracebridge Bay.

Inn at the Falls is known for its nostalgic charm, relaxed patio overlooking the Muskoka River and a new smart-casual restaurant that is a reflection of the property's entrancing character. Each of the inn's rooms and suites are unique, many sporting names of individuals with ties to the buildings and its former inhabitants. The one-time stables have been transformed into a furnishing and décor consignment space. Throughout the building are reminders of its long history: a 140-year-old fireplace still stands in what was once the parlor, sweeping up to the second floor is the original staircase and carved wooden bannister, and in the basement is evidence of the three-foot-thick foundation of locally-quarried stone.

Tip: If you're into the paranormal, consider staying in Room 105, the William Mullock Room. Tradition says this large room, with its raised, four-poster bed, is the most haunted in a building that has long been famed for its ghostly happenings. But for a real treat, opt for Room 101, the Mahaffy Suite, a two-floor unit with private balcony and a hint of extravagance.

Inn at the Falls dates to 1876.

Kawandag (Rosseau Lake College)

1967 Bright Street, Rosseau
Web: www.rosseaulakecollege.com
Email: School.office@rosseaulakecollege.com
Phone: 705-732-4351

Kawandag Lodge. The Eatons of department store fame had a cottage-mansion on the shores of Lake Rosseau.

Horrendous war cries erupt from the forest as fierce Indigenous warriors break from the foliage to storm a palisaded fort. The retort of musketry follows as the pent-up British red coats pour withering fire at the enemy. A cannon joins in the desperate defense, its deafening boom echoing across the waters of Lake Rosseau to startle people quite far away.

The history books say that war has never shattered the vaunted Muskoka tranquility, that no skirmishes were fought amongst its forest and lakes, but the history books are wrong. For two years, British soldiers fought against restive First Nation tribes in defense of Fort Kawandag, protecting the approaches to Rosseau.

Confused? Would it help if you knew those two years were 1965 and 1966, and the combatants were actually actors in one of Muskoka's most unique—if short-lived—tourist attractions.

Kawandag, an Ojibwe word meaning "the meeting place of the pines," began not as a fort but as the palatial summer estate of Sir John Eaton, famed founder of Eaton's Department Stores. In 1906, Sir John purchased a beautiful stretch of shoreline in Rosseau and had a grand, pillared summer cottage built. No expense was spared. Sir John hired Scottish stonemasons to build the foundations and fireplaces, and brought in craftsmen from Europe to complete the interior woodwork. The cottage had the latest amenities, including stables, a grand salon, music room, golf course and a room from which to watch the sun rise and another to watch the sun set.

After Sir John's death in 1922, Lady Eaton came to Kawandag less frequently, and she eventually decided to sell in 1945. For a time, Kawandag remained a private retreat, but in 1949, new owners Maurice and Lynette Margesson turned the cottage into a resort called Kawandag Lodge. It operated as such for more than a decade, but the size of the property and cost of upkeep proved prohibitive. With each passing year, Kawandag Lodge fell further into disrepair and the owners into financial ruin.

The resort was sold to entrepreneurs Maury East and Roger Morris in 1963. After three seasons of disappointing results at Kawandag Lodge, they decided they needed a fresh new approach. They hit upon the idea of building a western-style fort on the property where exciting battle skits could be performed. In an era when Daniel Boone was ruling the airwaves, it seemed like a great idea.

The fort measured 100 feet by 100 feet (30 metres), consisting of a 12-foot (3.7 metre) palisade of cedar poles sharpened at their top, enclosing four block-houses (one at each corner), a jail, tailor shop and a six-foot (two-metre) wide firing ramp supporting the cannon. The focal point of the inner courtyard was an authentically built birch-bark wigwam and a 15-foot (4.5 metre) totem pole made by Indigenous craftsmen. The former Eaton cottage served as the fictional governor's manor.

Indigenous tribal leaders were won over and many men and women from various regional Reserves—including Gibson and Rama—found employment there as re-enactors. The skit went to effort to portray First Nations in a positive light. Indeed, one of the heroes was Chief Yellowhead, a real figure who served the Crown loyally in the War of 1812 and the 1837 Mackenzie Rebellion.

Living history was just in its infancy, and this was as close as Muskoka had. The classic elegance of the old Eaton estate reinforced the illusion of a bygone time and place, and people were seduced by the sensation of travelling back to an era long past. More than 28,000 people passed through the gates that inaugural season, giving hope for a bright future.

Unfortunately, attendance declined substantially in the second year, and Fort Kawandag was surrendered—not to hostile warriors, but to market realities—after a mere two years.

In its place arose a more enduring enterprise, Rosseau Lake College private school. Founded in 1967, the school is an independent co-ed day and boarding school that offers students an alternative to conventional classroom study with a challenging academic program and engaging extra-curricular activities with an outdoor emphasis. It continues to thrive today with an international reputation for excellence.

Note: Sadly, in 1973 a fire destroyed the former Eaton mansion, which housed the school library and lounge, but a few outbuildings remain, including a log cabin that was once Lady Eaton's private retreat. Additionally, Lady Eaton's gardens still grace the campus.

LEWISHAM

Lewisham is located at the end of Lewisham Road, east of Barkway

The only building still standing to remind us of Lewisham is this one-time schoolhouse.

James Edward "Ted" Taverner arrived in Muskoka in a wagon holding the entirety of his worldly possessions. While driving along the rutted road, the grey skies overhead suddenly opened up and a cold rain fell. Taverner's toddler, Harold, sleeping fitfully in the wagon's bed, began to wail in discomfort. Taverner reached back and pulled a tarp over the shivering toddler, who quickly dozed again as the wagon continued to bump along.

Taverner's mood was as downcast as the weather. He silently prayed that his decision to move to Lewisham from Toronto was a wise one.

The epitome of a backwoods hamlet, Lewisham was always poor and somewhat primitive. The soil here is so poor that farmers could barely grow enough to sustain their families in the best of years and were supported almost entirely by employment with logging companies working in the area.

Despite his worries, Taverner was among the few to prosper. He established a steam-powered sawmill, had a farm which boasted a herd of 50 head of beef cattle (this in a community where having a chicken on the dinner table was a luxury) and ran the general store.

When the harvestable trees were denuded in the early 20th century, families literally abandoned their farms and fled. Even Taverner had to accept defeat, closing his businesses in the 1920s. Of the community only the schoolhouse (now used as a seasonal hunt camp) and the cemetery with a few lonely headstones remain, and of the four farm-lined roads that once made up the crossroads, three are now overgrown.

LIMBERLOST FOREST AND WILDLIFE RESERVE

1088 Buck Lake Road
No admission
Web: www.limberlostforest.com
Email: info@limberlostforest.com
Phone: 705-635-1584

Once a four-season resort, Limberlost is now an appealing wilderness park.

Limberlost Lodge defined the concept of a wilderness resort; it was as if the phrase "getting back to nature" was coined just to describe a stay at this resort located deep in the midst of virgin forests on the borders of Algonquin Park.

Limberlost was built in 1921 by Gordon Hill as a paradise for those with a passion for outdoor sports. The reserve boasts more than 300 kilometres (185 miles) of trails for hiking, biking, cross-country skiing and horse-back riding.

"The charm of the Limberlost country, deep in the forest," suggests an early promotional pamphlet, "is the maze of small lakes and streams, rocky wooded ridges, deserted clearings, saddle trails and old pioneer roads."

Limberlost was unique among Muskoka's resorts of the time in that it was open year-round, and it came to develop a particularly fine reputation for its winter sporting activities. In 1934, an 1800-foot (550-metre) long alpine ski hill, known as "the Top of the World" and occupying the highest elevation in Muskoka, was developed.

The resort boasted a main lodge with 13 guest rooms decorated in a rustic style, as well as a number of fishing camps. Limberlost had one of the largest stables in all of Muskoka, with more than 100 horses specifically trained for trail riding.

Today, Hill's original vision—a place where people can get close to nature—lives on in the form of Limberlost Forest and Wildlife Reserve, with more than 70 kilometres (44 miles) of hiking, biking, skiing and snowshoeing trails winding through 10,000 unspoiled acres of mixed forest and lakes.

LITTLE NORWAY

Muskoka Airport, 1011 Airport Rd, Gravenhurst
No Admission
Web: www.muskokaairport.com
Phone: 705-687-2194

Muskoka played host to the exiled Royal Norwegian Air Force during World War Two.

On April 9, 1940, Nazi Germany attacked neutral Norway with over 100,000 men. The unprepared Norwegian armed forces, equipped mostly with obsolete equipment and unprepared for war, had little hope of standing up to the invasion; even the intervention of an Anglo-French expeditionary force could not alter the outcome. By June 10, Norway officially surrendered. Previous to that, but only once the battle was no longer in doubt, King Haakon VII, his family and members of the government had fled the country aboard the cruiser HMS *Devonshire* to establish a government-in-exile in England.

Many Norwegians followed suit in order to continue the fight against the Nazis, either making the dangerous crossing of the North Sea aboard fishing boats or with British commandos returning from raids.

Despite the fact that their country was occupied, the Norwegians made a substantial contribution to the Allied victory in 1945. Thirteen vessels of the Royal Norwegian Navy escaped to England in June 1940, and by war's end, the Navy-in-exile had grown to 7,000 men and women crewing 50 ships. The huge Merchant Navy—38,000 men in 1,000 vessels—played a major role in the Battle of the Atlantic and a 4,000-man Norwegian Brigade helped to liberate their homeland in 1945.

The Norwegian air forces—the Army Air Service and Naval Air Service, later amalgamated into the Royal Norwegian Air Force—played a similarly importantly role in winning the war. A shattered force after the German invasion, it had to be painstakingly built up from scratch. Much of the work of revitalization was done in Muskoka, where thousands of pilots and air crews received their training at a facility known as Little Norway, located at Muskoka Airport just outside of Gravenhurst, a facility built in 1933 as a Depression-era "make work" project for unemployed men.

On May 1942, Muskoka Airport was leased to Norway and officially opened by Norway's Crown Prince Olav. An adjacent farm was purchased to expand the facilities, which grew to include three turf runways, hangars and a collection of log buildings reminiscent of those found in Norway to house airmen and support their training. The cost was born by the huge Norwegian merchant marine, one of the largest in the world.

The Norwegians also purchased a 430-acre recreational retreat east of Huntsville called Interlaken, now the Olympia Athletic Camp at Limberlost. To the Norwegians, it was known as "Vesle Skaugum," or "Home in the Woods," the name of the Norwegian King's residence. This facility was used primarily for rest and basic training.

The planes upon which the Norwegian pilots trained were donated to the Royal Norwegian Air Force by Scandinavian expatriates throughout Canada, the United States and South America, and each one was personally unveiled and dedicated by King Harald and his sisters, the Princesses Rahnhild and Astrid.

Training continued at Muskoka until February 1945, by which time it was clear the war in Europe was in its final act and that Norway would soon be liberated. The RNAF moved their camp to an air base in England in preparation for the final move back to its native land.

By the end of the war, 3300 Norwegian officers, air crew and ground personnel had been trained at Little Norway, and the Royal Norwegian Air Force contributed five squadrons to the Allied efforts against Nazi Germany. Over the course of the war, Norwegian air crews shot down more than 225 enemy fighters, while sinking six submarines and damaging five more. The contribution to victory was impressive and could not have been made had the RNAF not had a facility to rearm, retrain and reestablish itself.

After the Norwegians left, control of Muskoka Airport reverted to the Canadian Department of Defense, and the barracks at the south end of the airport became Beaver Creek Correctional Camp.

Though the RNAF left more than 70 years ago, Muskoka has not forgotten the fair-haired pilots who trained there. In 2007, a commemorative plaque and memorial stone, the Little Norway Memorial, was unveiled as a reminder of the close-bond forged between Muskoka and Norway and the small but vital way Little Norway played in helping secure victory over Hitler's Germany. Inside the terminal, a small museum room has a display that relates the history through photos, text and a short video.

Note: Norwegian servicemen recuperated and received physical training at Limberlost Lodge in northeast Muskoka, today known as Limberlost Forest and Wildlife Reserve. See pp. 106-107 for details.

LOOKOUT MOUNTAIN

Lookout Road, Huntsville
Admission Free

Stunning views of Fairy Lake from atop Huntsville's Lookout Mountain

At the top of Huntsville's Lookout Mountain is a popular spot that offers stunning views of Fairy Lake, especially in autumn with its backdrop of traffic-light reds, oranges and greens.

The lookout is also a place rich in local history. Alexander Murray named the lake for its beauty during his 1853 surveying trip but was beaten there by a number of years by Alexander Bailey, who opened a trading post at the foot of the mountain. A Métis man descended from fur traders, Bailey enjoyed excellent relations with the Indigenous people. One can almost imagine Alexander Bailey standing atop the rise and looking out onto the lake, watching for canoes laden with furs. He might then race down the mountain to his trading post located along the shoreline below where he exchanged tools, ammunition, food and clothing for furs.

When Muskoka was opened for settlement, Indigenous trappers had to go farther north for their furs, and Bailey abandoned his post. He moved first to Bracebridge, where he built that town's first sawmill and gristmill, then to Port Carling.

There is nothing left of the trading post, save for the spectacular views that Bailey once had all to himself before the region was opened for settlement.

MADILL UNITED CHURCH

Madill Church Road, just south of Huntsville

A fine example of square-timber log construction, Madill United Church dates to 1873.

Madill United Church, a beautiful square-timbered structure, serves as an enduring symbol of the community spirit that exemplified life in the 19th century on Ontario's frontier.

Settlers began to arrive in the Huntsville region in the mid-1860s. John and Matilda Madill were among the first. Life was harsh, so these settlers sought comfort in religion. At first, people held services within their own homes, but in time they built dedicated houses of worship. In 1872, with farms now firmly established, Madill donated land, and each member of the congregation donated two logs that were then squared, dovetailed and fitted together by volunteer labour.

The church was officially opened on May 8, 1873. The congregation was justifiably proud of what they had accomplished. Looking upon the fine structure, the settlers allowed themselves to imagine what else they could build, what they might yet accomplish in a region that just a few years prior was untamed wilderness. It represented a promise of what might come.

The Madill family remained devoted to the church throughout the years. In 1935, Madill's daughter, Agnes Armstrong, redecorated the building at her own expense. Later, she and her brother, Archie, unveiled a historic plaque on the grounds.

In recognition of its historic importance, the Madill Church was the recipient of a Muskoka Heritage Foundation Built and Cultural Heritage Stewardship award in 2007.

Trivia: Among those buried in the cemetery is Captain George Hunt, founder and namesake of Huntsville.

MARY LAKE

Muskoka Road 10, north end of Port Sydney

Mary Lake was named in 1853 by explorer Alexander Murray.

Of the seven largest lakes in Muskoka, Mary Lake is the least known and frequented. At one point, there were as many as 25 resorts on the lake. Today, only a handful remain active, leaving behind a sedate and seemingly unspoiled lake. Most of those who reside and cottage on its shores prefer it this way.

Alexander Murray explored this area in 1853 under the auspices of the Geological Survey. When he came upon a crystalline lake, he was so struck with its beauty that he named the lake after his eldest daughter, Mary.

There is some controversy surrounding the lake's naming. Everyone uses Mary Lake, and indeed this is the name recognized on all official documentation, but some old-timers insist this is all wrong. They insist, adamantly, that the name is actually Mary's Lake.

Eight islands dot the lake, with Port Sydney Beach (a great spot to swim and play on a hot summer's day and welcome reprieve from a driving tour) facing three of them not far offshore. The closest, in direct line with the government dock, is a clump of Canadian Shield appropriately called Rocky Island.

The central island, by contrast, is graceful in appearance. The smooth curve of its back reminded Indigenous peoples of a swimming otter, inspiring the name, *Kche-negeek-chiching*, or "Place of the Great Otter." Today this island, the largest on Mary Lake at 18-acres, is known as Crown Island. Some mistakenly believe it was named after the British monarchy because it was once crown land. In fact, it was named for a family headed by Edward Crown, who settled in Port Sydney in 1879.

The final isle facing Port Sydney Beach is known, simply and descriptively, as the Isle of Pines.

Launch a canoe or kayak to explore the lake's other islands.

The Three Sisters islands as seen from Port Sydney

The macabre-sounding Deadman's Island was originally part of the land grant of a career mariner named Captain Cock. Around 1869, 62-year-old Cock met beautiful and vivacious Emma Ladell, whose family had just emigrated from England to settle on the shores of Mary Lake. That summer, Emma became pregnant with Cock's baby, and the couple was quickly married that October, despite a 40-year age gap. They built a cabin on the island and had a contented life together that included raising six kids. Cock died in 1889 and, wanting to be surrounded by water for all eternity, specified in his will that he be buried on the island. The grieving widow followed his wishes. Thus: Deadman's Island.

Forrest (formerly Rumball's) Island is named after families who lived at the north end of the lake. The

Rumball family owned the island and the farm adjacent to it from 1873 to 1889. Since the island was deer free, it became essentially a giant vegetable plot. It was later sold to the Forrest family, and the name changed with the sale.

In 1869, William John Lawrence and his family took up land on the north end of Mary Lake, including the island now known as Lawrence Island. The oldest son, Charles Treffrey Lawrence, eventually took over the farm and married Lucy Crompton in 1878, the daughter of an Anglican minister instrumental in the building of 20 pioneer Anglican Churches in Muskoka.

The final landmass within Mary Lake is Gall Island, but locals generally call it Buckhorn Island since it lies just off Buckhorn Point. The origins of both names are mysterious. The island was never settled, nor was there a nearby landowner of either name.

MUSKOKA HERITAGE PLACE

88 Brunel Road
Admission
Web: www.muskokaheritageplace.com
Email: rgostlin@huntsville.ca
Phone: 705-789-7576, extension 3210

More than a dozen historic buildings from across the region are preserved within the recreated pioneer village at Muskoka Heritage Place.

Muskoka Heritage Place is the greatest repository of history in Cottage Country. Feast your eyes on the stunning array of 19th- and early 20th-century Muskoka artifacts—farming utensils, household goods, craftsmen's tool and clothing—within a museum detailing Muskoka's history. Then step out outside into a mock village comprised of more than a dozen buildings. Indeed, the buildings themselves are exhibits, having been moved here from other parts of Muskoka and restored to ensure their preservation, but combined, they demonstrate a typical pioneer community in the years 1860 to 1910. Visitors can step back in time and experience pioneer days virtually firsthand.

You'll begin your tour at the 1875 Wesley Methodist Church from Milford Bay. Perched prominently atop a hill overlooking the village, the Church continues to be used for weddings today. Not far away is another community structure, the Ashworth Hall, built by the ardently-Protestant Loyal Orange Lodge (L.O.L.). Although it later became a town hall and schoolhouse, the building has been furnished to reflect the era when secretive meetings of the gentleman's fraternity were held within. Marked by a tall flagpole and playful seesaw is the one-time Etwell schoolhouse, built in 1895 of hand-hewn logs.

Several pioneer homes lend a sense of how settlers once lived. The wood-framed, peaked-gabled Hill House is as quaint as they come. Built in 1874, it was the home of Reverend Robert Norton Hill, the first man to homestead the Hillside area (the community was named in his honor). A Methodist Minister and Justice of the Peace, Hill is best remembered for blazing a trail from Huntsville to Peninsula Lake in 1868, a route that has become modern-day Highway 60.

William Strong was born in Ash, Michigan, in 1838. He enlisted in the 9th Michigan Infantry during the Civil War and fought in a number of battles, including Chickamauga. William had four wives and eight kids, among them a daughter named Minnie, who married Nawton Marr, a settler in Novar (just north of Huntsville). In 1924, 86-year old Strong and his ailing wife, Hortense, went to live with the Marrs. Hortense died just nine days after arriving. Tragically, William died 10 months later after falling through a trapdoor and is buried in St. Mary's Cemetery in Novar.

Other examples of pioneer homes include the log Daniel Bray House and the tiny James Darling House, within which the settler and his wife somehow managed to raise nine children.

The Spence Inn is easily the largest building within the confines of Muskoka Heritage Place. Its size, the wrap-around porch and the grandeur of its furnishings indicate this was a building of importance. Built in 1878 alongside the Nipissing Colonization Road, which ran from the village of Rosseau in the south to Lake Nipissing in the north, the inn catered to road-weary travellers. Because it was located in the village of Spence roughly at the road's midway point, the establishment was named the Halfway House. One can easily imagine stagecoaches pulling up to the porch, as they did for decades.

Follow the scent of smoke and the loud ringing of metal upon metal to the village blacksmith where a spiritual descendant of the building's original artisan carries on his memory and trade. British-born Frank Gabriel was an impressive man. Apprenticed to a blacksmith at the age of 13, he so quickly became a master in the trade that by 15 he was helping to replace the frames of the stained-glass windows in London's Westminster Abbey. Immigrating to Canada, he settled in Novar in 1926, when blacksmiths were becoming increasingly rare and on the verge of obsolescence. But Frank Gabriel endured, defying the passage of time and crippling arthritis that permanently disfigured his legs. Shortly after his death in 1969, Gabriel's family donated his tools and smithy to Muskoka Heritage Place to educate modern visitors about the vital role these craftsmen played in the rural way of life.

The community general store was the department store of its day, selling everything a villager might reasonably need from farming utensils to foodstuffs, cloth to nails, and oil to sweets. They also served as post offices. Ned Hay ran his general store in Falkenburg for decades.

Muskoka Heritage Place hosts a number of unique events throughout the year, including Canada Day Celebrations with pioneer demonstrations and live music, an Easter Egg Hunt and the family-friendly Great Pumpkin Trail, with kids trick-or-treating among heritage buildings.

Visitors experience pioneer days—minus the backbreaking toil—firsthand at Muskoka Heritage Place.

Muskoka Lakes Farm and Winery

1074 Cranberry Road, Bala
No admission; fee for Bog to Bottle Tours and other activities
Web: www.cranberry.ca
Email: Ontario@cranberry.ca
Phone: 705-762-3203

Muskoka Lakes Farm and Winery, Ontario's only commercial cranberry farm and winery, has put Bala on the map.

The brilliance of fall in Muskoka is legendary. Ontario's woods are ablaze in fiery shades throughout October. As forests are being transformed into a colourful tapestry, harvest season is in full swing. Perhaps in no place does the bounty of the season— brilliantly coloured leaves and flavourful crops— come together more perfectly than in Muskoka, home to some of the best leaf-peeping in the province as well as our most distinctive fall crop, the crimson cranberry, floating languidly in their flooded fields.

With 11 hectares in cultivation producing 137,000 kilograms of cranberries each year, Johnston's Cranberry Marsh is the only existing cranberry farm in Ontario. It also boasts one of North America's only cranberry wineries. Of the visitors that explore the bogs and watch as cranberries are harvested or sample unique cranberry wines, few recognize the trials and tribulations, labour and expertise that has gone into transforming the wild wetlands into a thriving farm and Ontario landmark.

Let's start at the beginning. Cranberries are a native North American fruit that Indigenous tribes inhabiting Eastern Canada and the United States harvested and called "bitter berry." This harvest was vital to their winter survival; cranberries were mixed into pemmican, a small cake made of dried meat, to provide a source of vitamin C necessary for warding off scurvy. Indeed, cranberries were so important to their lifestyle that tribal legends tell of how they were a gift from the Great Spirit and sent to Earth in the beak of a dove.

When Europeans arrived in North America, they quickly saw the advantages of cranberries as well. Despite the fact that Ontario's Indigenous Peoples had been harvesting cranberries for centuries, there was no attempt to establish a commercial cranberry farm in Ontario until George Mollard established a short-lived one in MacTier in 1947. Working alongside Mollard and learning the ropes in the cranberry fields was Orville Johnston.

Three years later, Orville Johnston established a cranberry farm of his own just outside of Bala. Land was cleared, wetlands drained, and streams dammed almost entirely by hand. The early years were difficult and there was much trial and error involved, forcing Johnston to moonlight as a musician to make ends meet. But in time, with hard work and perseverance, the farm established firm footing.

Orrville's son Murray, along with his wife, Wendy, and their children, continue the much-expanded operation today. Since taking ownership, they have branched out and expanded the appeal of cranberries with Muskoka Lakes Winery. As a result of the decision to use only the choicest fruits and the uniqueness of their brands, Muskoka Lakes Winery has won numerous awards. Thanks in large part to their ongoing efforts, the cranberry has become synonymous with autumn in Muskoka, serving as the inspiration for the can't-miss Bala Cranberry Festival.

The biggest misconception about cranberries—and there are many—is that they are an aquatic plant. They actually grow in boggy fields. It was discovered that ripe cranberries float in water, and so it became common practice for farmers to flood fields in the autumn to facilitate harvesting. This is one of many fascinating facts you discover during the daily bog-to-bottle tours of the farm (recently named a Signature Canadian Experience).

In October you can watch as berries are harvested from the flooded fields, enjoy wagon rides of the bucolic property, wade in amongst the berries for a priceless photograph and sample a number of delicious cranberry wines. An autumn day at Johnston's Cranberry Marsh is a truly memorable experience.

But don't limit your explorations to an autumn day. During the summer, as cranberry flowers bloom on their vines, enjoy hiking trails or take part in a guided tour to Blueberry Hill with its scenic outlook, where you taste blueberry wine and discover facts and lore about this cousin of the cranberry. When snow descends on the farm, skate the ice trail, play bog hockey, strap on snowshoes and sip hot mulled wine and cider. Spring, of course, is maple syrup season. The Bog to Bottle Discovery tours have been designated a Canadian Signature Experience by the Canada Tourism Commission. For the price of admission and available year-round, visitors can participate in a guided farm tour followed by a tutored wine tasting.

Regardless of the season, Muskoka Lakes Farm and Winery offers a true taste of Cottage Country.

Muskoka Lakes Museum

100 Joseph St., Port Carling
Admission
Web: www.mlmuseum.com
Email: info@mlmuseum.com
Phone: 705-765-5367

No trip to Muskoka is complete without a visit to Muskoka Lakes Museum.

The pioneer spirit is quite literally at home on Island Park in Port Carling. Since 1967, Muskoka Lakes Museum in Port Carling has exhibited and interpreted the area's history. Even prior to that date, Island Park had a notable past.

In the 1920s and '30s, the island was a hive of activity. A government-operated fish hatchery raised trout to restock lakes that had seen fish stocks plummet as a result of pollution from sawmills (impressive concrete foundations can still be seen on the island's north waterline). There was a building with a pool hall on the ground floor and a movie theatre above, a boat livery that rented canoes and rowboats to tourists, a lawn bowling green, and baseball field (a large net prevented fly balls from hitting boats passing through the canals). For a time, W.J. Johnston operated his boatbuilding business here (more on him later).

By the 1960s, however, the glory days were long past, and the island was abandoned. When townspeople were looking for a place for a museum, they quickly realized Island Park was ideal—in the midst of the village but in a tranquil setting with plenty of grounds for hosting activities. On July 2, 1967, a ribbon was cut and the museum declared open.

The museum has proven so successful over the years that it necessitated a number of expansions. The most notable addition came in 1982, when the Hall House, a log cabin from Glen Orchard, was acquired. Painstakingly disassembled, removed from its original site and reconstructed on the island by volunteer labour, it has been furnished with artifacts to demonstrate the lifestyle of a typical Muskoka pioneer. Note the massive size of the logs—60 centimetres (24 inches) thick and 9 metres (30 feet) long.

You'll begin your tour in the gift shop, which among other things boasts a notable collection of local history books, then pass into the Resort Room, which is designed to convey the feeling of stepping into the lobby of a typical Muskoka resort in the early

20th century. There's an interactive switchboard telephone, and the walls are lined with reprints of old postcards from the region's many summer hotels, most of them long-gone.

The First Nation's Gallery is dedicated to the region's first inhabitants. A replica *wigwam*, two authentic birch-bark canoes and a range of artifacts demonstrate the traditional Ojibwe way of life. The gallery is particularly appropriate because traditional campgrounds were located just across the river. With the influx of tourists, the Ojibwe found a steady market for their beautifully handcrafted baskets and moccasins.

The Marine Room honours Port Carling's boat-building heritage with a range of outboard motors, dating to as early as 1916, and several impressive wooden boats. The most prominent artifact is a "Dippy," a rare example of a Disappearing Propeller Boat built by W.J. Johnston (who we met earlier). The son of Port Carling's founding father Benjamin Hardcastle Johnston, W.J. began building boats in 1869 and in the early 20th century founded the Disappearing Propeller Boat Company with his nephew W.J. Johnston Jr. The most distinctive feature of a Dippy, as the disappearing propeller boats were known, was a propeller shaft that was designed to fold up into its cast-iron housing should it hit a shoal or deadhead. By 1922 the company was the largest motorboat-building business in the British Empire and even had a branch plant in Tonawanda,

New York. Sadly, the company failed just a few short years later. Today, Dippies are among the most prized possessions in Muskoka.

Within the modern inventions room, visitors find old logging tools such as a 1930s chainsaw, a portable blacksmith's forge that would have likely been put to use in lumber camps in the winter and shoeing farmers' horses the remainder of the year, a hot air pump (one of only 12 in existence) and implements used by early, wealthy cottagers who demanded the comforts of home even while on vacation. The Marion Catto gallery, named for one of the museum founders, hosts the season's feature exhibit.

"The museum isn't just about preserving artifacts," asserts curator Doug Smith. "It's about telling the story of the community." To that end, throughout the operating season the museum engages the community through programming and special events including workshops, lectures, art shows and book launches.

Muskoka Steam Museum and Portage Flyer

100 Forbes Hill Drive, Huntsville
Admission
Web: www.muskokaheritageplace.ca
Email: ron.gostlin@huntsville.ca
Phone: 705-789-7576

At only a mile (1.6 km) long, the Portage Railway was the shortest railway in the world.

In 1875, a lock on the north branch of the Muskoka River ensured steamships could pass unhindered on Mary, Fairy and Vernon lakes. Peninsula Lake joined them in 1888 when a canal was dredged between it and Fairy Lake, and then there was Lake of Bays, the largest of the four, but isolated and inaccessible by boat. It was tantalizingly close, with just a mile of land separating it from Peninsula Lake, but it might as well have been 16 kilometres

(10 miles) because the elevation variance between the two was 51 metres (170 feet). Dredging was clearly not an option, and building a lock system would have proven prohibitively expensive. Lake of Bays seemed destined to be separated.

Contractors built a gravel road across the portage, and a local family, the Osbornes, put their farm horses and wagon to good use hauling passengers and freight across in a primitive taxi service. It worked, sure, but was slow, inconvenient and wouldn't appeal to wealthy individuals who might want to vacation at a Lake of Bays resort.

A better solution arose in 1903 when workers began laying narrow gauge tracks for a railway linking the two lakes, from North Portage at the far end of Peninsula Lake to South Portage on Lake of Bays. When it began operating a year later, the Portage Railway was officially the world's shortest commercial rail service. Suddenly, vacationers had a comfortable and dignified mode of transportation; without the Portage Flyer (as the train was called) such lavish resorts as the Britannia Inn, WaWa Hotel and Bigwin Inn wouldn't have developed. And in addition to passengers, the Flyer also provided transport for mail and all matter of cargo.

The Portage Railway operated successfully for almost six decades, but when the last steamship ceased sailing in 1958, the railway was suddenly without purpose. It closed, its rolling stock sold off, and its tracks lifted.

Thankfully, while the Portage Railway was gone, it wasn't forgotten. In the 1990s the Portage Flyer was located in St. Thomas, Ontario, where it had been operating as the Pinnafore Railway for decades. The train was purchased and returned home to Muskoka. Today, it once more bears vacationers, this time on brief scenic excursions.

Your experience begins at Rotary Village Station, a faithful re-creation of a typical 1920s Ontario train station. Inside you'll find a museum explaining the important role steam travel played in opening up the area to settlement, tourism, industry and development. You can then hop aboard the Portage Flyer and settle into one of two authentic open-air coaches, the Algonquin or Iroquois, both named for steamships that once plied these waters in connection to the Portage Railway, and head out on a scenic trip along the Muskoka River. The tracks end at Fairy Lake Station, which was originally the steamship Pursor's Cabin at Norway Point on Lake of Bays. Stretch your legs briefly and then board once more for the return trip. The entire excursion is a pleasurable 30 minutes.

In the busy summer season, the locomotive pulling the flyer is an authentic 1926 steam engine, one of only a handful still operating in Ontario. While this engine was owned by the Portage Railway, it proved too heavy for the light gauge rails and caused them to bend. Consequently, it spent most of its previous career in an engine shed. In the shoulder-seasons, a 1949 diesel electric locomotive that was employed in the pulp and paper industry in New-foundland takes over.

Note: The Portage Railway's original line is largely overgrown, and with each year the former railbed becomes more and more difficult to discern. However, the landing at South Portage allows you to connect with the railway's past. The tranquility of this location belies the bustling activity of yesteryear when steamships pulled up along wharves piled high with freight and crowded with passengers, when piles of lumber and tanbark lined the shores nearby. A line of evergreen trees alongside North Portage Road marks the route the railway took down to the wharf, where the tiny train would pull out right onto the dock to disgorge and pick up passengers and cargo.

Portage Flyer is a Muskoka treasure.

Muskoka Wharf

Highway 169, Gravenhurst (Muskoka Wharf) or
  275 Steamship Bay Road, Gravenhurst (Muskoka Discovery Centre)
No Admission (Muskoka Wharf) or
  Admission (Muskoka Discovery Centre)
Web: www.gravenhurstchamber.com (Muskoka Wharf) or
  www.realmuskoka.com (Muskoka Discovery Centre)
Email: info@gravenhurstchamber.com (Muskoka Wharf) or
  info@realmuskoka.com
Phone: 705-687-4432 (Muskoka Wharf) or
  705-687-2115 (Muskoka Discovery Centre)

Perhaps no place in Muskoka is more appealing, or more historically significant, than Muskoka Wharf in Gravenhurst.

The shores of Gravenhurst Bay are alive with excitement not seen since the heady days when Gravenhurst was known as the Gateway to Muskoka. Flanked on the east by the Muskoka Steamships ticket offices and on the west by a Residence Inn, the bay's shore—known as Muskoka Wharf with shops and restaurants and boardwalk in between—is one of the coolest places to be in the region.

It is also a place rich in history.

Sagamo Parkette

Opened in 1986 on land beside Muskoka Steamships' dock and ticket office, Sagamo Parkette offers
shaded picnic tables, benches overlooking the water
and manicured gardens. It is a popular place for
picnic lunches and weddings.

In years past, however, it was a place of industry,
not recreation. For nearly a century, this same area
was the shipyard of the Muskoka Lakes Navigation
Company, where vessels were built or pulled up on
dry land for repair. It was a tangled maze of rickety
docks, weathered boathouses, storage sheds, lumber
and heaps of worn-out machinery. Thankfully,
Sagamo Parkette has succeeded in eliminating all
evidence of this industrial wasteland.

Greavette Boatworks

The site, once occupied by one of Canada's most
important boatbuilders, is buried under modern-day
Highway 169. A protégé of boatbuilding pioneer
Henry Ditchburn, Tom Greavette, set out on his own
in Gravenhurst. His company, Greavette Boatworks,
was one of the first boat manufacturers in Canada to
try assembly-line construction. The Depression made
Greavette's ambitious plans little more than a pipe-
dream, so instead he turned to the custom-designed
boats that would make him famous. Miss Canada IV,
built for Muskoka racing legend Harold Wilson, was
the fastest boat of her day, achieving speeds of over
200 mph (322 kmh). During World War Two, Greavette built 40-foot (12-metre) rescue boats for the
Royal Canadian Air Force.

After Greavette died in 1958, the company passed through various hands and was moved to Port Carling and ultimately closed. In 1987, the former Greavette Boats building in Gravenhurst was torn down.

New Muskoka Wharf

Today, the shoreline of Muskoka Bay is lined with boardwalks, restaurants and cafés, shopping venues, gazebos with pleasing views and heritage plaques—all part of the ambitious Muskoka Wharf development that has transformed a moribund stretch of lakefront into a vibrant tourist attraction. On any given day it is alive with activity: couples strolling hand-in-hand, boats coming in to dock and diners engaged in lively conversation over drinks and good food.

If one were to travel back in time 80 years or so, you would find activity of an entirely different sort here and the views far less appealing. During the heyday of lumbering (1870s to 1940s), almost a dozen sawmills lined the bay. The reek of smoke hung heavily in the air, and the whine of saws slicing through wood would have been deafening. You would see stockpiles of lumber and shingles and mounds of sawdust as far as eye could see, and out on the bay, the water was a tangled mass of thousands of logs.

Ditchburn Boat Manufacturing Company

Henry Ditchburn was the undisputed father of boatbuilding in Muskoka. He came from a long line of boat builders and, after settling in Rosseau in

1869, began making rowboats for the short-lived Rosseau House Hotel.

He moved his company to Gravenhurst, where he tutored most of the region's next generation of boat-builders and crafted luxury yachts for millionaires, such as the *Kawandag* for Sir John Eaton in 1916. Sadly, the company crashed during the Depression and closed in 1938. Today, the site of the Ditchburn Boat Manufacturing Company is occupied by the Residence Inn, which boasts 44 suites, all with balconies overlooking the water.

Muskoka Discovery Centre

For much more information on these locations, go to the Muskoka Discovery Centre. A state of the art museum, it has an outstanding collection of exhibitions on the history of Muskoka, focusing on steamships and resorts, as well as wooden boats, Indigenous peoples and early settlement. Perhaps more important, it's just plain engrossing, with a number of interactive exhibits sure to maintain the interest of even the youngest visitors.

The high for many is the collection of in-water antique wooden boats, the largest of its kind in North America. Others are attracted to the exhibit on the ill-fated Waome, which tells of Muskoka's largest maritime disaster, or the opportunity to step into the lobby of a recreated resort of yesteryear.

Norman Bethune Memorial House: Birthplace of a Canadian Hero

297 John Street N., Gravenhurst
Admission
Web: www.pc.gc.ca
Email: pc.bethune.pc@Canada.ca
Phone: 705-687-4261

Norman Bethune Memorial House. Dr. Norman Bethune is a hero both in Canada and China.

Bethune Memorial House was the childhood home of Dr. Norman Bethune, a man who was recognized as a figure of National Historic Significance in 1972. "Bethune is the most famous Canadian in the world, but his fame lies almost exclusively outside Canada," explains Site Coordinator Scott Davidson. "He's best known for his role in China, where he provided medical care during the Chinese war with Japan, but Bethune should be better known in Canada for his medical advances and commitment to health care here."

Bethune Memorial House was the manse of Knox Presbyterian Church. Bethune was born there in 1890 while his father, Malcolm, a reverend, was preaching at the church. Bethune lived there for three years, until his father was assigned another ministry and the family moved.

Bethune studied medicine at the University of Toronto but suspended his studies to enlist in the Canadian Army Medical Corps as a stretcher bearer during World War One. Wounded at the Battle of Ypres, he returned to Canada, finished his medical degree, graduated in 1916, and then re-enlisted with the Royal Navy. He later rose to become the first chief medical officer of the newly formed Royal Canadian Air Force by 1919.

In 1926, Bethune, with a thriving practice, contracted tuberculosis and returned to his hometown to seek treatment at Calydor Sanatorium. He spent six weeks there and wasn't expected to survive. Frustrated with conventional treatments, Bethune demanded he receive artificial pneumothorax, a dangerous operation that pumps air into the chest. When he survived and made a rapid recovery, Bethune decided to focus on tuberculosis.

Bethune then dedicated his career to fighting poverty because he believed that poverty bred illness and disease. He provided free health care in his

Montreal practice and pushed for free public health care across Canada many years before universal health care was introduced in the country.

When the Spanish Civil War erupted in 1936, he once again put aside his practice to serve the victims of conflict by offering aid to the Nationalist side. There, he put together the world's first mobile, battle-front blood transfusion service.

After Spain, Bethune travelled to China in 1938 to render medical assistance to Chinese forces fighting the invading Japanese. He designed a mobile medical facility that could be carried entirely on mules, published booklets to educate the Chinese about first aid and sanitation and began training dozens of nurses and doctors to spread his knowledge. Tragically, Bethune died a year later of blood poisoning contracted from treating a wounded soldier. Because of the tireless work he did in their country during the war, Norman Bethune is still revered in China and thousands visit the Memorial House every year.

Parks Canada purchased Bethune's childhood home, returning it to its turn-of-the-century appearance to reflect Bethune's time there. As visitors make their way through the house, exhibits and artifacts illustrate Bethune's life and accomplishments, including many pieces of medical equipment the man personally used. In an adjoining visitor centre, visitors can watch a biographical video on Bethune.

The grounds haven't been ignored by Parks Canada. They, too, have been restored to reflect the gardens and Victorian landscape aesthetics of a typical middle-class home in the late 19th century. Even here there are nods to Bethune; bloodroot and lungwort flowers line the front and sides of the house, symbolizing his work in blood transfusion and tuberculosis treatment.

A new addition to the grounds is a recreated World War One trench. Unveiled on Canada Day 2017 to honour the centennial of two of the most significant events for Canadians during the war— the battles of Vimy Ridge and Passchendaele—the trench is intended to be an immersive child-friendly exhibit where kids can gain a sense of a typical World War One battlefield and wear a lab coat and fake war helmets to learn to be a stretcher-bearer like Bethune.

Statue of Norman Bethune outside the museum

Oxtongue Rapids

Oxtongue Rapids Park Road (off Highway 35)
No Admission

In a remote corner of Muskoka, Oxtongue Rapids is worth a visit for its natural spectacle. It also hides a tragic tale.

In the remote eastern reaches of Muskoka, hidden in the dense forests along a rarely travelled, little-more-than-a-dirt-trail road, lies one of the region's most picturesque spots. Although photogenic at any time of year, it becomes even more spectacular in autumn when the forest is transformed into a patchwork quilt of oranges, reds, and yellows.

This is Oxtongue Rapids, a 3.2 kilometre (2-mile) stretch of turbulence along the primeval Oxtongue River, which flows from Oxtongue Lake down towards Lake of Bays.

Getting to the rapids is a bit of an adventure. At times, while driving Oxtongue Rapids Park Road, the trees seem to encroach upon you, reaching over top to form a dense canopy of foliage. The road cuts through sandy banks, which are the remnants of deltas left by the prehistoric precursor of the Oxtongue River. As glaciers retreated across the landscape, ice melt swelled the river to almost unimaginable levels, and the raging waters literally molded the terrain you drive through.

Eventually, you'll reach the Lion's Club Park. Here, and at various points further along, you'll be treated with stopping points that offer scenic vantage points overlooking the raging and boiling river.

Farther along the road is a cairn erected by the Dwight Lion's Club in the memory of Lloyd Bradley and Ralph Blackwell, two gentlemen whose vision and efforts contributed to the creation of the park. Just below the cairn, down a steep gravel road that is best walked owing to frequent washouts, is Hunter's Bridge. Although it's almost unknown today, the bridge has historical significance.

The Bobcaygeon Road was one of a number of colonization roads carved through the wilderness in the mid-19th century to open the hinterlands up to settlement. The Bobcaygeon Road was to run from Bobcaygeon to North Bay, a distance of about 220 kilometres (140 miles). Construction began in 1856, and by 1863 had advanced as far as the Oxtongue River. That was as far as it would go as the road was never completed; Hunter's Bridge marks the end of the Bobcaygeon Road.

Logs were once sent down the Oxtongue River by the thousands.

Later, a sideroad was built connecting the Bobcaygeon Road with the Muskoka Colonization Road via a route that more or less follows modern-day Highway 60 along the eastern shores of Fairy Lake, Peninsula Lake and Lake of Bays.

Hunter's Bridge was named for Isaac Hunter, a tragic figure if ever there was one. Hunter settled there with his wife in the early 1860s. Folklore says that Hunter took up arms with William Lyon Mackenzie and other insurgents of the ill-fated 1837 Rebellion, and that he had retreated to the then-wilderness around Dorset to flee prosecution. As the region was settled, Hunter—fearing persecution should he be recognized—retreated to the very limits of the Bobcaygeon Road.

But there's one problem with this tale: Queen Victoria issued a blanket amnesty for everyone involved in the rebellion. Even firebrand ringleader

Mackenzie was allowed to return from hiding in the United States and went on to pursue a political career. So Hunter, a mere follower, had no reason to hide beyond the reaches of civilization—but why let facts get in the way of a good story?

The story doesn't end there. Hunter died in his cabin during a particularly severe winter. Zachariah Cole, the founder of Dorset, happened upon the snow-bound cabin while travelling the road one blustery day. Seeking shelter for the night, he pushed open the door and made the grisly discovery: Hunter's starved body was being devoured by mice, which his emaciated wife and daughter, on the fringe of lunacy, were desperately trying to catch for food.

The horror of this tale doesn't detract from the beauty of the scene as the raging Oxtongue River cascades past. In a way, the story enhances it. In a setting where the power of nature is so prominently displayed, the sad story reminds us that we are so very often at nature's mercy.

PAIGNTON HOUSE/JW MARRIOTT THE ROSSEAU MUSKOKA RESORT

1050 Paignton House Rd., Minett
Web: www.marriott.com
Phone: 705-765-1900

JW Marriott The Rosseau Muskoka Resort and Spa is Marriott's gift to Muskoka. It carries on the proud legacy of an earlier resort, Paignton House.

Marriott's gift to Cottage Country, the JW Marriott Rosseau Muskoka Resort and Spa, rises like a majestic cruise liner over Lake Rosseau. This relaxed, yet elegant five-star hotel is a spectacular place to vacation. While the resort is a recent addition to the Muskoka region, the scenic property has been attracting vacationers since the 1880s, when John Frederick Pain opened his farmhouse to hunters and anglers.

Pain was born in India in 1845, the son of a wealthy English merchant. While growing up there, he contracted malaria and suffered from its effects throughout his life. In fact, it's been suggested that the chronic effects of the illness were directly responsible for Pain's arrival in Muskoka. His parents, so the story goes, listened to the advice of a physician and shipped their 21-year-old son to Canada in 1866 in the belief that Muskoka's fresh air and invigorating climate would restore his fragile constitution. But that is just one possible explanation for how Pain arrived in Muskoka; another theory put forward was that he was a troublesome young man and was sent to Canada by his father to distance him from some unknown scandal.

Whatever circumstances led Pain to Muskoka, he undoubtedly made his parents proud with what he accomplished there. The resort he founded, Paignton House (named after a town in England where his family lived), was among the most popular and enduring in the region. It was probably inevitable that someone would build a resort there. Ask any developer, and he will tell you this property is among the finest in Muskoka, with gorgeous sandy beaches and memorable views out onto Lake Rosseau.

Pain, it should be said, whether due to his fragile constitution or general disposition, wasn't much of a worker. Much of the credit for Paignton House's early success must go to his wife, Charlotte Pain. While J.F. was the face of the hotel, a sociable fellow who spent much of his days entertaining guests, his wife quietly worked behind the scenes to make sure everything functioned smoothly, that rooms were

Paignton House, early 20th century

cleaned, great food was served on time and the farm provided. She was tireless.

Thankfully, their heir, Dick, was the best of both of his parents. He was every bit as hospitable as J.F. but financed expansions and updates by toiling in Cobalt silver mines during the winter months when the resort was closed. He also put more acreage under cultivation so that Paignton House remained self-sufficient.

Dick's hard work ensured the resort remained viable to be passed onto the third generation. While many resorts were closing in the post-World War Two era, Paignton House—under Archie Pain—reached its apogee, becoming a beloved family-friendly destination with the tagline "Family Run for Family Fun."

However, more than a century of tradition at Paignton House came to a sudden end in 2000—about 30 years after passing from Pain family hands—when it was razed by fire and subsequently demolished.

One can't help but miss the Paignton House, with his rich history and its family-atmosphere, but what replaced the aging property was something more dramatic and spectacular, a place worthy of new memories. With diverse dining options, a luxuriant spa, waterfront activities for the entire family and a spectacular indoor-outdoor pool, the resort is, in every respect, magical. You will tire before running out of things to occupy your attention.

JW Marriott The Rosseau Muskoka Resort and Spa has been busy lately. In 2018 and 2019, the resort was given a fresh makeover, led by Toronto design firm mackaywong, to celebrate 10 years since it opened to acclaim. Always beautiful, the resort is now next level. The new look is sleek and contemporary—chic chairs and shiny lighting—yet retains an authentic Muskoka vibe thanks to innovative nods to the region's character, such as light fixtures reminiscent of deer antlers and carpeting reminiscent of Georgian Bay's windswept rocky shores. The most dramatic feature, however, is the stunning light fixture illu-minating the lobby, which brings to mind a flock of geese flying around a glorious Muskoka sun and, beneath it, a swirling wooden bench that looks like a massive, elegant piece of driftwood.

Book a room. You'll thank yourself.

Patterson-Kaye Resort

1360 Golden Beach Road
Web: www.pattersonkayeresort.com
Email: info@pattersonkayeresort.com
Phone: 705-645-4169

The main lodge at PK (as long-time guests refer to the resort) dates to the 1930s. Look for the stunning stone fireplace within.

For 80 years, Patterson-Kaye Resort (formerly Patterson-Kaye Lodge) has been a Muskoka stalwart. At one time, there were more than 100 resorts of various shapes and sizes vying for their share of the tourists that flocked to Muskoka each summer. That number has dwindled to a mere handful today, yet Patterson-Kaye (or PK to those who know it best) has endured and thrived.

PK opened on July 1, 1937. At first, guests stayed in bedrooms on the lodge's second floor, but within a few years demand saw a number of cottages built along the waterfront, and each one is still standing. Fresh laundry was delivered weekly by a young Gordon Lightfoot, whose music career was still far in the future.

In 1960 the resort was purchased by Frank Miller, the future Premier of Ontario. Miller changed the focus from wealthy couples to young families with kids and established traditions that lasted for decades, including Talent Night, with guests and staff alike participating, and calling guests to meals with the ringing of a bell. By 1975, PK was being run by 19-year-old Norm Miller, who would follow his father into politics as MPP.

The resort passed from Miller hands in 2005 and has been owned by Regalton Hotels and Resorts since 2015. Yet in many ways, PK is a throwback to simpler, nostalgic days. That is part of its charm.

Note: The main lodge no longer has guest rooms but instead houses the Four Seasons restaurant. Within the main lodge is the iconic stone fireplace, which has stood since 1936.

Peninsula Canal

Canal Road at the Muskoka River, Hunstville

Now used by pleasure boats, the Peninsula Canal was once plied by steamships.

Roads throughout early Muskoka were primitive, rutted affairs that often turned into quagmires after any significant rainfall. The only reliable form of transportation—save for the slender lifeline that was the railway linking Huntsville, Bracebridge and Gravenhurst to points farther north and south—was by steamship. Cheap and reliable, steamships carried the burden of Muskoka's early industry and passenger traffic in their holds.

In 1875, a lock on the north branch of the Muskoka River linked navigation on Mary, Fairy and Vernon Lakes, but left out Peninsula Lake. People began to call for a canal linking Peninsula Lake to the other three lakes.

One of those outspoken voices was Captain Alfred Denton, who operated steamships on these lakes and would eventually form the Huntsville and Lake of Bays Transportation Company. He recognized that a canal accessing Peninsula Lake would open up its shores to tourism, settlement and logging. In other words, he saw dollar signs.

Thankfully for Denton, the government agreed to finance a canal. They even found the ideal spot: a small creek, flanked by wetlands, that flowed between Peninsula and Fairy lakes. The soil was soft and wet, so widening and deepening the creek seemed eminently doable.

Dredging began in 1886. Excavation of the three-quarter-mile-long waterway cost $25,000 and took two years to complete. As predicted, the completed canal was a boon to the region, and it remains in use today.

Note: Enjoy a spectacular view of the Peninsula Canal from the patio of Deerhurst Resort's The Antler Steakhouse (www.deerhurst.ca) while enjoying great food.

THE PORT CARLING LOCKS

Highway 118 as it crosses the Indian River in the heart of Port Carling

Port Carling is known as the Hub of the Lakes. The locks are the reason why.

The village of Port Carling is known as The Hub of the Lakes. Watercraft of any size, from jetskis to steamships, that wish to pass between Lake Rosseau and Lake Muskoka must come through here—or more specifically, the locks located here. On a hot summer day there is a genuine bustle in this charming village as tourists flock here to admire the spectacle of passenger craft and steamships such as the RMS *Segwun* or *Wenonah II* passing through.

The locks are considered something of an engineering marvel and, while certainly still very much in use, they serve as a reminder of the important role water transportation played in Muskoka's development.

When settlers first arrived in what would be Port Carling, they discovered shoals and the Baisong Rapids in the Indian River that linked the two lakes. These represented an obstacle to navigation, and therefore the settlement and economic development of the region. Passengers and cargo would have to disembark steamships, portage across to Lake Rosseau and reembark. It was a time-consuming process. Worse, it could be dangerous because, before the removal of shoals in the Indian River, steamships could not get close enough to the shoreline to allow passengers to disembark directly onto docks. Instead, vessels would have to anchor offshore and extend a lengthy gangplank. While members of the crew held down one end, passengers carefully walked across this makeshift bridge and then jumped ashore. More than one person lost their balance and had to be fished from the water.

A.P. Cockburn, founder of the Muskoka Navigation Company and a Muskoka representative in provincial government, pressed for a navigational lock at Port Carling. He found an ally in John Carling, Minister of Public Works, and together they managed to get the project approved. His urgings were successful, and construction began in 1869. The need for extensive blasting made construction time-consuming, so it wasn't until November 1871 that the lock opened for navigation. As predicted, the locks were a boon to the development of the region.

A swing bridge once spanned the lock.

Tourism flourished, and resorts began to spring up like trilliums in a springtime forest. One example was the Polar Star Hotel, later known as Port Carling House, which sat astride the locks where a row of modern shops sit today. Opened the same year as the locks, the hotel welcomed guests for 80 years before the aging structure was torn down in 1970.

The locks remain in use today, though they have been expanded and rebuilt several times since, and electric gates have been installed to speed up the procedure from 30 minutes to a mere 10 today. Watching boats pass through is exciting, and the sides of the locks are always thronged with onlookers in the summer. It is easy to see why Port Carling is known as The Hub of the Lakes.

Many people don't realize that there are actually two locks in Port Carling. The other lock, built in 1921 and known as the small lock, is on the other side of the island and used specifically for small pleasure craft.

The bridge spanning the lock is a considerable engineering feat in itself. After all, it had to be designed to allow for even steamships to pass. The original bridge, built in 1875, was a wooden swing bridge. By 1921, the bridge was in desperate need of replacement. Instead of wood, the new swing bridge was made of steel.

The current bridge, which opened in 1973, is a departure from the original: it is a cantilever bridge that rises to let steamships pass. The grand-opening opening of the new bridge was set on a hot July 3rd day. Hundreds of locals and seasonal residents turned out to see the bridge raised for the first time, and Ministry of Transportation officials were on hand to cut the ribbons and bask in the glow of work well done. But when the bridge began to rise, the crowd gasped in shock as the asphalt began to slide down like black ooze. Officials were red-faced, the onlookers a blend of horrified and amused. It would be two more months before the bridge finally opened to traffic.

Note: Port Carling is the home port of Sunset Cruises' *Peerless II*, a beautifully restored supply boat that now offers scenic cruises of the lakes. *Peerless II* takes passengers into nooks and crannies where the larger scenic vessels simply can't.

Port Sandfield Canal and Bridge

Muskoka Road 7, at the heart of Port Sandfield

Started in 1870, the canal at Port Sandfield linked Lakes Rosseau and Joseph. Beautiful Prospect House once sat alongside it.

The canal and the bridge that span it are iconic to the little community of Port Sandfield. Each year, thousands of drivers patiently await their turn to cross this single-lane span, and for generations people have gathered in its shadow to watch steamships and pleasure craft pass beneath.

At one time there wasn't even a canal at Port Sandfield. Instead, Lake Rosseau and Lake Joseph were separated by a narrow spit of sand that blocked navigation. For many years, people crossing from one lake to the other were forced to portage across the sand (one entrepreneurial family even rented out their team of horses to haul boats across the spit), but if Lake Joseph was ever going to develop with farms, communities and resorts, a more efficient link was needed.

With that in mind, The Public Works Department stared dredging a canal at Port Sandfield in 1870. Later that year, a government delegation headed by John Carling, Commissioner of Public Works, and Premier John Sandfield came to inspect progress. They slept the night in tents and named the spot in honour of the premier. The words Port Sandfield were carved into a wooden plank and nailed to a tree.

The canal's opening in the autumn of 1871 was inauspicious: the steamer *Wenonah* got stuck during the official ceremonies. Another round of dredging was required for steamships to safely pass through. The canal was completed the following spring.

Sandfield Canal was a blessing for navigation, but it effectively cut the community in half, separating neighbours from one another. After fielding complaints for a number of years, in 1876 a wooden bridge was built over the canal. Because steamships had to pass underneath, the bridge was unusually—and unsettlingly—tall. People had to climb about 18 metres (60 feet) up and then build up the courage to cross to the other side. Some were simply too

Prospect House, one of the finest resorts of its day, burned down in 1916.

afraid to make the journey, especially when the all-wood bridge developed an unnerving sway after only a few years. The bridge was also impassible to horses and wagons. After enduring this misery for two decades, a wooden swing bridge was built in 1897. Finally, all parties—steamship captains, pedestrians and wagon-drivers alike—were appeased.

A few years after the original bridge had been built, Enoch Cox arrived on the scene and opened a 25-guest boarding house on the northeast side of the canal. Business boomed, and Cox then built a stately resort named Prospect House. By 1888, the ever-expanding hotel had grown to accommodate 300 guests and boasted a ballroom, music room and lawn bowling greens. As one of the largest and most refined Muskoka resorts of its day, Prospect House put Port Sandfield on the tourist map, drawing wealthy guests from as far afield as the United States each summer.

Sadly, this magnificent resort burned to the ground on October 15, 1916. With hardly any insurance coverage, Prospect House wasn't rebuilt. It was a real blow to the tiny community that relied on the resort to draw tourists.

Meanwhile, the wooden swing bridge was aging badly. In 1924, this second bridge was replaced by a metal swing bridge, which lasted for the better part of the 20th century. When it opened for the final time on September 6th, 1997, in a ceremony that saw the historic steam yacht *Wanda III* (once the property of the Eaton family of department store fame) pass through, it was the last hand-swung bridge in Ontario. Replacing it was the current hydraulic bridge, which opened the following year.

Pleasure boats and, on occasion, steamships still pass through the locks and under the bridge. In the summer, crowds laze on the shaded banks to watch as the watercraft pass and meander along the boardwalk that stretches from one lake to the other to take in the scenic vistas. A handful of shops on the north shore are well-worth poking into.

PORT SYDNEY SCENIC DAM AND FALLS

Foot of Ontario Street, Port Sydney
Admission free

Port Sydney Dam and Falls is a pleasant place for a stroll and pictures in the heart of Port Sydney.

The village of Port Sydney looks to British immigrant Albert Sydney-Smith as its founding father. He visited the area in 1871 and, like so many modern visitors, was immediately taken with the waterfall that empties out of Mary Lake into the Muskoka River. While today people admire the scenic beauty of the water as it glides over an incline of bedrock to form a natural waterslide (indeed, it may be Muskoka's only "slide-class" waterfall), Sydney-Smith recognized the industrial potential in the site.

The enterprising gentleman snapped up the land abandoned by the area's first settler, John McAlpine, which included a small sawmill at the waterfall. Smith enlarged the sawmill so that it had the capacity to cut 10,000 board feet of lumber per day, and then added a grist mill. Syndey-Smith subdivided his land in 1873, and a village—named Port Sydney in his honour—grew in the shadow of his thriving mills.

The mills are long gone (demolished in 1930), but the falls remain at the heart of the community. On a hot summer day, throngs of people gather on the wide, flat rocks at the waterfall's edge to paddle in the river and enjoy the sound of the babbling water. Few know that the rocks they sit upon were once an island, with water flowing on both sides, or that it was once the site of a sawmill. Just above the falls is a dam, which you can walk out onto for scenic views downstream and out to Mary Lake.

ROSELAWN LODGE

1041 River Street, Bala

Anne of Green Gables author LM Montgomery vacationed at Roselawn Lodge.

Roselawn Lodge, founded by Thomas Burgess Jr. (son of Bala founder Thomas Burgess) in 1903, may have lacked the name recognition or opulence of other Muskoka resorts, but it endured for decades and created many lifetimes worth of memories.

Anne of Green Gables author, Lucy Maud Montgomery, vacationed here for two weeks in 1922 and fell in love with the property, writing:

"The situation here is very lovely. The lawn runs down to the river where the bank is fringed by trees. It is beautiful at all times but especially at night when the river silvers under the moon, the lights of the cottages twinkle out in the woods along the opposite bank, bonfires blaze with all the old allure of the camp fire, and music and laughter drift across from the innumerable canoes and launches on the river."

It was while resting comfortably in a chair on the porch at Roselawn that Montgomery dreamed up her next novel, *The Blue Castle*, which many critics argue was her best.

A fire in 1941 claimed the lodge's main building, but other buildings on the property survived, allowing the resort to continue on for many more decades under the guidance of new owners, Fred and Mabel Nation, and later their son, Edward. Whether by coincidence or not, one summer in the late 1990s the theatric Follows family—including Megan, who had brought Anne of Green Gables to life on television—stayed at Roselawn for a month while performing at the Gravenhurst Opera House.

Today, Roselawn is a beautiful private cottage owned by a descendant of Thomas Burgess. It's so well preserved that Montgomery would likely still feel right at home.

Rosseau Falls

The falls are located on Rosseau Road 3, about 1.5 kilometres (.9 miles) from Highway 141.

You'd never know it, but a massive sawmill once operated at the foot of scenic Rosseau Falls.

A trip to Rosseau Falls is a must for any autumn leaf-peeping weekend or early spring outing when you're feeling a bit of cabin fever. As waterfalls go, it is not Muskoka's biggest, but it is by far one of its best. The Rosseau River runs serenely from Long Lake for 18 kilometres (11 miles) before pouring into Lake Rosseau through a tempestuous 150-metre (492-foot) long chute. It is a spectacular natural scene with raging water tumbling over large rocks, back-dropped by a panoramic vista.

In years past, a tiny hamlet once huddled around the base of the falls. In 1877, Peter Mutchenbacker built a sawmill and shingle mill here. Each spring thereafter, logs that had been cut in the heavily forested interior over the preceding winter were sent barreling down the river to gather in the lake below. After the spring drive, the bay was packed so tightly with logs that one could quite literally walk from one shore to the next without getting wet feet. In the shadow of the mill stood several cabins housing the families of the mill hands, a store with a post office and a number of farms. The mills operated until the 1920s, after which the town withered away.

Frenzied activity is long gone, replaced by serene beauty. Stop at the bridge and walk along the river's banks for a panoramic view of the falls and distant lake. While the water slows to a trickle during dry summers, in spring and autumn it is transformed into a frothing beauty.

Tip: There are actually two waterfalls on the Rosseau River. Don't overlook the 5-metre (16-foot) high cascade on the south side of Highway 141.

Rosseau General Store

1 Rice Street (corner of Rice Street and Highway 141, Rosseau
Phone: 705-732-4479
Web: www.rosseaugeneralstore.ca
Admission free

Rosseau General Store has been a landmark in Rosseau since 1874; it is a must visit.

For 140 years, the Rosseau General Store has stood at the heart of its community, a village landmark that has watched as Rosseau experienced ebbs and flows in its fortunes, a constant in good times and in bad. A remarkable heritage structure, it is the oldest continuously operating general store in Muskoka and one of the oldest anywhere in Ontario.

The store exudes nostalgic charm. The architecture speaks of another era, a time when horse and wagons rumbled along muddy roads and when the local economy was based not upon tourism but farming and logging. The front steps have been worn thin by the boots and shoes of thousands of feet over the years. Every footfall, every stair taken, carries you decades back in time. By the time you enter the store, you might as well be in the 19th century. If you listen carefully, the aged floorboards groaning underneath whisper tales of ages long past.

The first tale would speak of the store's construction in 1874. At that time, there wasn't much in Rosseau. The community was founded in 1863 with the arrival of British Bill (Albert Williams) and Edward Clifford and, even 11 years later, was still a true frontier village, huddled alongside Lake Rosseau and pressed in on the shores by an imposing wilderness. A handful of homes belonged to settlers desperately trying to scratch a living from the rocky soil. The only luxuries of civilization were to be found at the general store built atop the hill in town by the Peacocks (of whom little is known). These founding owners lasted only a short period, but they laid the foundation for one of Ontario's oldest continuously operating general stores.

Edward Jordan is the first owner we know much about. A distinguished English gentleman with a long shock of black hair bearding his face, Jordan lasted until about 1887 and transformed the store into a thriving small-town enterprise. Succeeding Jordan as owner were Homer and Co., Jerry Little and, from 1922, James Brown. James and his wife

A cattle-drawn (!) carriage outside the store around the turn of the 20th century

Freda were beloved members of the community and did much to expand their business, most notably the purchase of a small steamship, *Constance*, for use as a floating store to serve cottages and resorts along the lake.

The Rosseau General Store became the heart of the small community. It was a place where you could purchase just about anything one could reasonably desire, from candy and foodstuffs to clothing, farm utensils, tools and ammunition. It was the village department store. But more than that, the store was a social centre where people gathered to share news, tell tall tales and create the tight bonds for which small towns are known. In the winter, people huddled around the big pot-belly stove, while in the summer they lounged in the shade of the long verandah. Regardless of the season, "going to the store" meant a welcome reprieve from a physically demanding life to relax for a few moments with friends.

A succession of owners followed the Browns over the decades. The one trait they all had in common was a respect for the history they inherited. While village life has changed dramatically over the years, the general store has been lovingly maintained and few physical changes made. It is still the place you can buy pretty much anything you need; the porch still offers welcome shade perfect for chatting amiably, and the proprietors are as warm and welcoming as ever.

Anyone who visits the Rosseau General Store, who listens as the floorboards creak and groan underfoot, marvels at the 19th-century architecture and snaps photos of a joyful vacation, is thankful for the foresight and care exhibited by the various owners over the past 140 years. Thanks to them, the building remains an authentic old-fashioned country store and one of Muskoka's historic treasures.

After more than 140 years in service, the Rosseau General Store has lost none of its charm.

Rosseau Memorial Community Hall

2 Victoria Street West, Rosseau (corner of Victoria Street West and Highway 141)

Rosseau Memorial Community Hall, built with local rock, commemorates the village's World War veterans.

For the village of Rosseau, the scale of loss in World War One was too unbearable to be simply forgotten even after the guns had fallen silent late in 1918. Of the 90 Rosseau and area men who had served in uniform, 10 would not return from the distant battlefields.

These devastating casualty figures had a profound impact on Reverend Joe Ditchburn. It was important to Ditchburn that the community find a way to both help heal wounds and honour the sacrifice of the fallen. Around 1921 inspiration struck. For decades, the Orange Lodge had played host to almost every community function of note, but by the 1920s Rosseau had long outgrown the Lodge. A new, dedicated community hall was clearly required. Ditchburn hit on the idea of building an impressive new hall, one which would serve as a memorial "to the boys from this area who served and died in World War One."

Sir John Eaton of Eaton's department store fame, whose cottage was located in Rosseau, generously paid for his personal architect to draw up plans for the proposed hall. Concrete foundations were poured in 1923, at which time a cornerstone was laid by Ditchburn. Throughout that year, field-stone was gathered by volunteers and then painstak-ingly hauled to town by horse-drawn wagon. Cutting and laying stones is a skilled task, so a stonemason was hired to do the work.

A moving opening ceremony was held on the afternoon of August 27, 1924, during which granite memorial tablets embedded on the building's front wall and inscribed with the names of the men from Humphrey, Cardwell and Watt Townships were unveiled. The bugle's lament played the "Last Post," the gathered sang "God Save the King" as the flag was raised to half-mast on a nearby flagpole, and then a somber one-minute's silence was observed.

The hall was used as a meeting place for all community associations, including the Women's Institute, Lions Club, and Agricultural Society and for all manner of town functions, ranging from political rallies, weddings and dances to school Christmas

concerts and travelling vaudeville shows. As antici-
pated, the Memorial Hall became the beating heart
of Rosseau's social and community life.

There were a range of strict rules in place that
reflected the distinct morals of the time. All dancing
must end by 12 PM, alcohol could not be served
within the hall; and no one under the influence of
alcohol could enter the building. All public meetings
must be conducted in an orderly fashion. Smoking,
spitting, swearing and whistling during performances—even to voice one's approval—were strictly
forbidden. To ensure that these rules were followed,
at least two board members were on hand during
every public event.

A mere generation after the Memorial Hall opened,
there was another global war into which Canada was
again drawn. As before, numerous men from Rosseau and its environs answered the call to serve, and
far too many died on foreign battlefields only to leave
gaping wounds in the tight-knit community. On the
afternoon of May 8, 1949, residents of Rosseau once
again a gathered at the Memorial Hall to pay homage
to those who had kissed their families goodbye to
fight fascism. In a ceremony far smaller but no less
moving than that in 1924, a bronze tablet bearing
the names those who had fallen in World War Two
was unveiled, and a scroll bearing the names of all
those who served in these wars hung inside.

Renovations were completed in 2004, ensuring
the Rosseau Memorial Hall would continue to play

a prominent role in the village into a new century. It continues to play host to events for the whole community, including movie nights, meetings of the Rosseau Historical Society and Horticultural Society, and wedding receptions. A public library is housed in the basement.

With its unique field-stone walls, historical atmosphere and memorial plaque that provide graphic illustration of the bitter cost of war, the Rosseau Memorial Hall is a special building—one beloved by residents and cottagers alike.

Note: A plaque dedicated to the Nipissing Colonization Road, which ran more than 100 kilometres (60 miles) from Lake Rosseau to Lake Nipissing to encourage settlement, has been placed at the hall.

The hall celebrates its centennial in 2024.

Santa's Village

1624 Golden Beach Road
Admission
Web: www.santasvillage.ca
Email: information@santasvillage.ca
Phone: 705-645-2512

Inside Santa's Cottage. Muskoka's theme park, Santa's Village, is more than 60 years old and proudly preserves its history.

Santa's elves have been busy. Not only have they been tirelessly crafting toys at their North Pole workshop for all the good children (and really, aren't they all good?), but they have also been pulling double shifts the last two years building new attractions at St. Nick's summer home, Santa's Village, in Bracebridge.

The resulting additions to the cottage-country theme park has made it more immersive, more exciting and more welcoming for visitors—both children and their parents alike. While much has changed at Santa's Village in the 60 years since it opened, much has also stayed the same. There are historical nods to the early years of Santa's Village throughout the park, each one with a colourful story to share.

Bracebridge in the 1950s was a town in crisis. The closing of the Bird Woollen Mill, the town's largest employer, and the rerouting of Highway 11, completely bypassing Bracebridge and thereby depriving local businesses of tourist dollars, had undermined Bracebridge's fortunes. Concerned citizens began casting about for a way to put Bracebridge back on the map; they needed an attraction that would lure people to town. Someone came up with the idea of a Santa-themed park that would be billed as Santa's summer home, in keeping with Muskoka's "cottage country" identity. Everyone agreed that Bracebridge was the ideal place for such an attraction since it was located on the 45th parallel—exactly halfway between the Equator and the North Pole.

Santa's Village was an instant hit with the public. The grand opening of the park in 1955 (the same year, incidentally, as Walt Disney World opened in California) saw then-premier Leslie Frost and Marilyn Bell, fresh off her milestone swim across Lake Ontario, cut the ceremonial ribbon. Bell also swam the 4.8 kilometres (3 miles) from Bracebridge to the park in the chilly May waters of the Muskoka River.

Several structures from that inaugural season still stand, including Santa's cottage, the wishing well (the coins collected were originally used to purchase toys for underprivileged children) and the hilltop chapel. Inside the chapel is a nativity scene, reverently displayed with hymns and carols playing softly in the background, just as it was back in 1955. The chapel is sanctified holy ground and has even hosted a wedding (appropriately enough, the bride and groom were staff members that would later portray Mr. and Mrs. Claus). Its bell comes from an early Bracebridge schoolhouse.

Originally, entertainment included quaint nursery rhyme skits, wagon rides and barnyard animals. The Candy Cane Express—still a highlight of the park today—was among the first rides added. It made its debut in 1956 at the Eaton's Toyland, located on the sixth floor of the department store at Yonge and Queen in Toronto. After a few years of chattering through the toy department with cars filled with exuberant children, the Candy Cane Express was sold to Santa's Village. There's an interesting footnote to the Candy Cane Express story: Bracebridge native Roger Crozier served as engineer of the train for several summers before going on to an illustrious hockey career with the Detroit Red Wings.

While the Candy Cane Express might have been the most popular ride purchased from Eaton's Toyland, it wasn't the only one. Also purchased at the time were a tiny Ferris wheel and a whimsical merry-go-round, which still entertains little ones to this day.

In the gift shop, you'll notice merchandise depicting a Husky named Snowbo. This is a nostalgic nod to yesteryear. The early Santa's Village went to great lengths to promote Snowbo, Santa's dog. He was prominent in advertising, and a whole line of Snowbo merchandise was developed to take advantage of their one intellectual property: "Snowbo is a trademark of the village and will probably become more familiar to Canadian children than Rudolph," opined the *Toronto Globe* in 1956. While the *Globe* was a bit off the mark in just how popular the beloved dog would become, Snowbo would indeed evolve into an iconic part of Santa's Village with generations of children who loved saying hello to him as he lazed by Santa's cottage.

It is impossible to compare the modern Santa's Village to that which emerged in the Enchanted Forest just outside of Bracebridge in 1955. Over the past six decades technology has advanced, tastes of children have evolved and the park has broadened its focus to cater to a much wider target audience. One thing has remained the same despite the many changes: the youthful joy of Christmas lives on at Santa's Village, creating a place of pure magic where anything, and everything, seems possible.

Segwun/Muskoka Steamships

185 Cherokee Lane, Gravenhurst
Admission by cruise
Web: www.realmuskoka.com
Phone: 1-705-687-6667

If one image is more synonymous with Muskoka it almost certainly would be RMS *Segwun*, the coal-powered steamship that has been sailing these waters since 1887.

If Muskoka is known for anything, it's for crystalline lakes sparkling in the sunshine. There are more than 1600 lakes in all, each one an irresistible lure. They are the spirit of the cottage lifestyle—from swimming to fishing to boating and waterskiing, most of our favorite activities centre on water.

It is therefore fitting that among Muskoka's most recognizable icons are her steamships, *Segwun* and *Wenonah II*. These twin vessels offer visitors, many hailing from the other side of the globe, with another angle from which to view the region's prized lakes.

In the early 1860s, when the first settlers began trickling into Muskoka, they found a landscape that was full of rocky outcroppings, dense forest and extensive swamps that made overland travel difficult. In the absence of good roads, the region's extensive waterways became the transportation arteries binding Muskoka together.

The first to see this was visionary entrepreneur Alexander Peter (better known as A.P.) Cockburn, who visited Muskoka for the first time in 1865 and immediately fell in love with its natural splendor. He also recognized its potential for exploitation by settlers and lumbermen. In the years that followed, Cockburn became Muskoka's greatest champion. In 1866, he launched the first steamboat in Muskoka, the *Wenonah*, an 80-foot (25-metre) sidewheeler that proved a godsend to the region's early settlers, encouraging settlement, industry and commerce.

He added more steamships to his growing fleet, including the *Nipissing* in 1871. This vessel burned and sank in 1886 while at anchor at Port Cockburn (divers claim her skeleton can still be seen in the depths just offshore), but was quickly replaced by the much improved *Nipissing II*, the first iron-hulled steamer to sail on any of Ontario's inland waterways. After extensive alterations in 1925, the *Nipissing II* was renamed RMS *Segwun*, the very vessel that takes enthralled passengers on cruises today. Today, RMS *Segwun* is the oldest Royal Mail Ship in the world, the oldest commercial vessel in Canada and the seventh oldest steamship in world.

But in 1958, *Segwun* ceased sailing, the last of a once-vast fleet of steamships to ply the Muskoka

Lakes. She sat idle along the wharves in Gravenhurst for many years, and people began to despair of her fate. Thankfully, her potential as a tourist attraction was recognized, and fundraising and restoration began in the 1970s.

June 27th, 1981, was a historic day for Muskoka, when the steamship era on the Muskoka Lakes returned with the maiden voyage of the painstakingly restored RMS *Segwun*. She proved so successful and iconic an attraction for not only Muskoka but all of Canada, that just over a decade later demand for cruises was surpassing capacity. She needed a partner. The result was *Wenonah II*, a modern-built ship that nonetheless manages to retain a Victorian-era charm. *Wenonah II* towers over her older sister and has a capacity of 200 passengers, double that of the *Segwun*, and boasts modern amenities (foremost an elevator for accessibility).

Today, operated by the Muskoka Steamship Association on behalf of the Muskoka Steamship and Historical Society, the vessels are among Canada's foremost tourist attractions. They are the perfect tandem, *Wenonah II* representing the future and *Segwun* a nostalgic nod to the past.

For a touch of romance, opt for the Sunset Dinner Cruises where you enjoy a three-course meal before retiring to the main deck to enjoy live entertainment as you soak in the spectacular view of the orange sun dipping below the horizon and reflecting off the crystalline water. The four-hour Millionaire's Row Tour, which has been designated a Canadian Signature

Experience, takes passengers back to the early 20th century by travelling to the original turn of the century cottages of Millionaire's Row in Beaumaris, which were owned by some of the richest families in Canada and the United States.

Finally, a number of child-centric cruises are hosted all season long aboard *Wenonah II*, including Pirate Cruises, Princess Cruises, Civic Holiday Fireworks and ending with a Halloween Cruise.

A cruise aboard RMS *Sewgun* or *Wenonah II* transports you back in time.

Note: Don't overlook the great gift shop at the steamship's ticket office and the outdoor displays (including a coal hop, used to deliver coal to the steamships).

RMS *Segwun* as *Nipissing II*

Sherwood Inn

1090 Sherwood Road
www.sherwoodinn.ca
Email: sherwoodreservations@clublink.ca
Phone: 705-765-3131

Designed to reflect a comfortable Muskoka cottage, Sherwood Inn is a charmingly intimate resort with a proud past.

Guests of Sherwood Inn are lulled back in time. Since it was founded by Toronto lawyer Harry Draper in 1939, Sherwood Inn has been perfecting the art of hospitality. Guests at Sherwood Inn have come to expect crisp white linens, access to an extensive wine cellar boasting more than 100 labels, gorgeous views over a pine-draped property gently flowing down to the waters of Lake Joseph and world-class cuisine that is both sophisticated and comforting at the same time.

Draper built the resort to more closely resemble a New England manor than a resort. It was intended to be a place where personal service and intimacy meet; he wanted guests to feel as if they were staying at a friend's cottage.

Over the course of its 80 years, Sherwood Inn has seen its share of history unfold and is the host to countless stories. There was the time Harry's son, Charlie, apprehended two would-be-thieves at gunpoint during a raging snowstorm, or the time rapper Snoop Dogg was hurriedly moved from his secluded cottage to other accommodations when he became unnerved by the stygian blackness of the Muskoka night. Then there was the desperate search for Princess Alexandra when her boat disappeared during a sightseeing cruise on Lake Joseph. (Spoiler alert: She was found, and everything turned out fine.)

Artists frequently found inspiration in Sherwood's natural splendour. Lawren Harris, a member of the Group of Seven, was a frequent guest. So, too, was George Thomson, brother of the ill-fated Group of Seven painter Tom Thomson and a talented artist in his own right. On several occasions Thomson painted at Sherwood; one of his oil paintings remains in the Draper family to this day, proudly hanging at the family cottage.

Sherwood Inn passed from the Draper family in 1962, and a number of owners have come and gone over the years. The most recognizable was Milt Conway, a TV personality for CKVR in Barrie, who hosted several popular shows, including *Romper Room, Strike it Rich, Reach for the Top* and *Captain Foghorn*. Conway operated the resort for many successful years in the 1970s.

A devastating fire in 2009 nearly cost Cottage Country another of its precious historic resorts. Quick-thinking staff managed to get all guests out safely, and fast-acting fire crews contained the fire to the dining room, lounge and lobby. Incredibly, a wedding scheduled for that coming weekend proceeded; a beautiful ceremony was held on the lawn, and the bride and groom took photos within the fire-blackened remains of the lobby.

If Draper were able to visit the resort today, he wouldn't feel out of place. The main lodge, authentically restored after the fire, is still nestled snuggly among century-old pines. Cottages dating back to the 1950s still dot the grounds. The little home where Charlie Draper and his wife raised Harry's grandchildren—today housing conference rooms—overlooks the lodge from atop a rise.

The tradition of excellence in hospitality, accommodations, food and facilities that has been a part of Sherwood Inn's history is still very much alive. The illusion of timelessness is so complete, one might expect to see a steamship packed with visitors pull up to the dock, just as it would have in years past when the primary means of arrival was by water.

That isn't to say Sherwood Inn is dated, however. Under Clublink ownership, the resort is among the finest in Muskoka. Recent renovations (largely necessitated by the fire) have entered the property into the 21st century. The most impressive addition is a basement wine room, available as a private dining area for groups of up to 14 people. Surrounded by 2000 bottles from more than 220 different wine labels, and with its exposed brick walls and intimate lighting, it is an elegant and exciting place to enjoy a meal. This unique Muskoka dining experience is a fitting addition as Sherwood has been honoured with the Wine Spectator's Award of Excellence on numerous occasions.

Note: Prior to 1939, Sherwood's property was the home to Edgewood, a homestead-turned-boarding house that opened its doors to guests starting in 1905. Its name lives on in the form of a Sherwood cottage, located about where the boarding house stood. If one pushes aside the undergrowth and looks carefully enough, the aged foundations can still be found alongside the modern cottage.

Lawn bowling on the grounds of Sherwood Inn

South Falls

Muskoka Falls Road, north of Highway 118. Park on the river on the right side of the road

South Falls Log Chute, circa 1900. Legendary explorer David Thompson made the first mention of this thundering waterfall in his 1837 journals.

The first Muskoka waterfall to be seen by European eyes was South Falls. Lieutenant Henry Biscoe of the Royal Engineers discovered the falls in 1826 during the first recorded exploration of Muskoka. Legendary explorer David Thompson made the first written mention of this waterfall in his 1837 journals during an expedition intended to determine the feasibility of a canal route between Georgian Bay and the Ottawa River.

At 33 metres (108 feet) South Falls, also known as Muskoka Falls, is the highest waterfall in Muskoka.

It may also be its most powerful; the river has cut an 800-metre-long (2600-foot-long) chasm in the bedrock.

While impressive to behold, this gorge proved an impediment to lumbermen driving their logs downriver to lumber mills in Lake Muskoka. Many were damaged by the rocks or wedged into crevasses, creating logjams. In 1878, the Ontario government built a 1000-foot-long (305-metre-long) log slide to carry the logs past the turbulent falls. Its grand opening drew crowds of onlookers but was marred by tragedy when a foolish workman jumped aboard the first logs sent down the slide and was killed. The slide remained in use until the 1930s.

The Town of Gravenhurst built a generating station at the base of the falls in 1907, and the facilities were later taken over and expanded upon by Ontario Hydro. Sadly, the plant and the sluice pipes that feed it disrupt the majesty of the setting, but the sheer power of the water is impressive, nonetheless.

Note: The best views of the falls are from the bridge over the river.

St. James Church
191 Hotchkiss St., Gravenhurst

St. James of Gravenhurst recently celebrated 150 years.

With its bell tower rising above the streets of Gravenhurst and its tolls echoing through town during times of celebration and mourning, St. James Anglican Church has been a distinctive part of the community for more than 150 years.

The Anglican congregation of St. James was established in 1865 while Gravenhurst was still in its infancy. Early services were conducted in a log tavern—the Freeman's Arms—belonging to James McCabe. McCabe later sold the congregation a parcel of land on Manitoba Street on the south end of town (where St. James Cemetery is located today) for the construction of a dedicated church.

By 1877, the village had developed farther north on the Muskoka Road than McCabe or any of the early church leaders had expected. St. James, consequently, was just too far away, so plans were made to build a new church within the confines of the village. Dugald Brown, a wealthy hotelier and son-in-law of the architect of the original church, provided land on the corner of Hotchkiss and John streets upon which to build.

Unfortunately, worshippers didn't have long to enjoy the new church; a fire in 1887 devastated much of Gravenhurst and completely enveloped St. James. When the smoke cleared, tearful congregants saw there was nothing left of the church but burning red embers and fire-blackened timbers. Once again, they would have to rebuild.

The third St. James, rising from the ashes of its predecessor, held its first services on September 30, 1888. This building boasts a prominent bell tower, housing a 700-pound (320-kilogram) bell donated by the Ladies Aid Society (which continues to be rung today), and beautifully crafted interior woodwork.

St. James represents one of the finest examples of Victorian church architecture in Muskoka.

St. John the Baptist Church

1233 Juddhaven Road, Morinus

St. John the Baptist Church is one of the most picturesque sights on Lake Rosseau.

What St. John the Baptist Church in Morinus lacks in physical size, it makes up for in historical stature and aesthetic allure.

In 1899, settler William McNaughton gave lakeside land to the Roman Catholic mission for the construction of a church. Over the next two years, the congregation raised the necessary funds, and on July 22, 1902 the church was officially blessed by Bishop O'Connor.

The completed church was, and remains today, one of the most attractive churches in Muskoka. Located atop a rocky bluff and overlooking Lake Rosseau, with its clean white frame outlined against bright blue skies and twin spires reaching toward the heavens above, St. John is an inspiring sight (especially from the water below, by which most worshippers would have arrived in the early years when travel along the primitive roads was trying and time consuming).

Pause here on your road trip for a few moments of calm, and admire the workmanship and pious decor of this sanctuary.

Tip: Walk down to the wharf (many people continue to come by boat for Sunday mass, just as they did a century ago) and look to your right. You'll see the rocky outcrop called Victoria Rock. It is said to resemble the profile of Queen Victoria from a certain angle.

St. Michael's Church

1168 Highway 141, Rosseau

St. Michael's Catholic Church was once part of Monteith House.

There's little about Rosseau's St. Michael's Roman Catholic Church that tells of its rich heritage. The church is a modest wooden building of simple construction and little ornamentation. The church looks more like a cabin than a house of God. That's because the building that now houses St. Michaels once belonged to Monteith House, the finest resort in Rosseau.

Monteith House traces its roots back to 1865 as a roadside hotel catering to weary travellers. Thirteen years later, John Monteith bought the hotel, turned its attention to summer vacationers and expanded it greatly to accommodate several hundred vacationers. Montieth House developed a reputation for outstanding food.

Monteith House

Monteith raised sheep on the property to provide lamb for guests (thanks in part to Monteith House, Muskoka lamb became a delicacy served at the finest restaurants in Toronto and beyond). The lambs were butchered on-site in a building purposefully built for the task. It is this building that is now St. Michael's.

In 1938, Harry Shopsowitz, founder of the famous Shopsy's Delicatessen in Toronto, purchased the resort as a place where Jews—unwelcome in most Muskoka resorts at the time—could spend their summers in relaxed luxury. The resort prospered as never before, necessitating additional accommodations to keep pace with demand. The former butcher shop was converted into guest rooms.

On November 15, 1950, Montieth House burned down. The butcher shop survived and, after interior remodeling, found new purpose as a Catholic church.

Torrance Crypt

1032 East Bay Road (1 kilometre/.9 miles north of Highway 169)

Eerie Torrance Vault is a reflection of the tragedies endured by the Whiting family.

Standing silent and sentinel over a field of gravestones in the Torrance Cemetery, the Torrance Crypt is a haunting burial vault with an equally haunting story behind it.

William Odell Paul Whiting was born in England in 1859 and came to Canada in the 1870s. In 1892, Whiting purchased a large property on Lake Muskoka and began to build a hotel he hoped would be among the finest in Cottage Country. Whiting spared no expense so that, when the Brighton Beach Hotel opened in July 1895, it was a vision of elegance and grandeur. It was the largest on the lake.

Sadly, the Brighton Beach Hotel never saw any guests. One week after officially opening, a fire razed the building. Whiting was understandably heartbroken. His dreams were shattered. The only consolation was that no one was hurt.

In time, Whiting decided to rebuild, but he didn't have the money to replicate the opulence of his first resort, so the second Brighton Beach Hotel was more modest in scale and outfitting. Opening in 1898, the Brighton Beach Hotel welcomed wealthy guests every summer until May 17, 1917, when it too was destroyed by flames. Unlike the first fire, in this one there was a casualty: Whiting's infant granddaughter.

The loss of a beloved granddaughter and the financial ruin of two major fires proved too much for Whiting. He never rebuilt and never fully recovered.

William Whiting, still heartbroken, died in 1937. He, along with wife Clara and two of their children, are buried in the haunting stone crypt in Torrance.

Note: Look for a plaque here revealing the first school in Woods Township stood on this site

Wilsons Falls

The falls are found at the end of River Street in Bracebridge.

Wilsons Falls is the most unspoiled waterfall in Bracebridge, which is known for its waterfalls.

The smallest of the three waterfalls within the municipality of Bracebridge, Wilsons Falls is ranked by many as their favourite because of the ease of exploration and the tranquility surrounding it. It is also the most undisturbed. Unlike Bracebridge Falls and High Falls, human touch is far less noticeable here. True, a small hydroelectric station built in 1909 stands along the river, generating electricity for Bracebridge, but it is remarkably unobtrusive and doesn't really detract from the pleasing scene.

In fact, there are two falls here. The main waterfall is a mere five metres (16 feet) high but an impressive 100 metres (330 feet) wide, likely making it the broadest waterfall in all of Muskoka. The second waterfall—the higher of the two—is located beside the red brick building that houses the generating plant.

After enjoying the falls, take some time exploring the setting. Walking trails (which connect to the Trans-Canada Trail) wind through the woods, and a boardwalk guides visitors along the picturesque banks of the Muskoka River above the falls.

Like all of Muskoka's waterfalls, the power of Wilsons Falls was harnessed by early settlers; in this case, namesake Gilman Wilson who, together with early settler William Holditch (postmaster in the nearby ghost town of Falkenburg), built a sawmill here in the 1870s that endured for decades.

WINDERMERE HOUSE

2508 Windermere Rd., Windermere
Web: www.windermerehouse.com
Email: info@windermerehouse.com
Call: 705-769-3611

Stately Windermere House is one of Muskoka's iconic images.

There are few places in Muskoka quainter than the village of Windermere, with the elegant Windermere House standing squarely at its heart. The resort roots the village firmly in the past—one look at its expansive porch and twin towers and you're transported back to the gilded Victorian age—while its modern luxuries serves to attract tourists.

Scotsman Thomas Aitken arrived in Muskoka in 1860, and built a log shanty where the fourth green of the Windermere Golf and Country Club is located today. A few years later, he moved closer to the lake and built a new home on a rise overlooking Lake Rosseau. This home evolved into Windermere House. Despite a personality that was described as "dark and taciturn," Aitken soon found himself running a thriving resort that would, over time, become one of the iconic images of Muskoka.

His son Leslie and daughter Gertrude took over after Thomas' death and were responsible for making Windermere a resort of elegance and refinement. They sold land for the creation of Windermere Golf and Country Club, updated the furnishings, bought the finest china and glassware and added a beauty parlour to appeal to the high-class guests increasingly demanding greater services. Mrs. Timothy Eaton, wife of the millionaire founder of Eaton's Department Store, was a frequent client of the parlour and was well known for being demanding and impatient.

Another celebrated guest was World War One flying ace William "Billy" Bishop, who would fly up from Toronto by float plane. During his stay he would offer other guests scenic flights, and for a time, Bishop even operated an air passenger service—the first in Canada— that brought guests to Muskoka in record time.

The resort passed from Aitken hands in 1981, but the change in ownership by no means saw Windermere's fortunes dim. Watch carefully in the 1985 Anne of Green Gables series starring Megan Follows; you'll notice Windermere House filling in for the fictional White Sands Hotel. Hollywood came calling again a decade later, when location managers arrived in Muskoka in search of an old-style hotel to serve as a setting for an action film, *A Long Kiss Goodnight*, starring Geena Davis and Samuel L. Jackson. Windermere was ultimately chosen, but sadly the resort burned to the ground during filming.

The community mourned the loss, but thankfully Windermere's owners believed they had a duty not only to rebuild, but to do so as faithfully as possible. The new Windermere House, a virtual carbon copy of the original from outside, reopened on May 31, 1997, with Premier Mike Harris signing the register as the first official guest. A tradition was restored.

Windermere House blends nostalgia with luxury in a seamless package. Here, guests indulge in fine food, luxuriate in comfort and enjoy the waterfront and golfing at Windermere Golf Club—one of the oldest in Muskoka. For a taste of history, guests can also enjoy a brief walk through the quaint hamlet that envelopes the resort.

Behind the resort is Christ Church, over 100 years old with hand-crafted doors. Looming over the rustic church is the resort's old water tower, dating back to the 1920s.

Farther on, you come to Windermere United Church, built in 1950, which contains a memorial window commemorating the Aitkens and other families that contributed greatly to Windermere's development. On the other side of Windermere Road, just to the south, sits a squat concrete building. This was originally used as a garage by Charlie Roper to house and service guests' cars. In later years, it became the Windermere House laundry and is today a maintenance building.

Finally, across from the resort, down by the waterfront, are the exclusive Windermere Cottages fractional units. This was once property belonging to the Fife family. Settler David Fife was Thomas Aitken's brother-in-law. In 1889, David Fife Jr. built a resort of his own in this very spot. Fife House was a popular destination in its own right for decades, but was later absorbed by Windermere House and then, in recent memory, torn down to make way for modern development.

All told, this insightful walk through 150 years of Windermere history would take approximately an hour.

Guests rode in carriages from the steamship wharf to the hotel.

WINDSOR PARK

3070 Muskoka District Road (Highway) 169, Bala
Admission free
Waterski Show: Tuesdays at 7:30 in July and August (www.
summerwatersports.com)

Windsor Park was once home to the Windsor Hotel, a fine summer resort that burned in 1907. Its successor, the New Windsor Hotel, was demolished in 1969.

For decades people have been gathering in Bala's Windsor Park on warm summer evenings to watch in awe at the spectacle of waterskiing performed by members of the Canadian National Ski Show Team and put on by Summer Water Sports (SWS), Canada's leading water sports entertainment company. It is a thrilling show that has become iconic to this small village (other weekly SWS shows are held at Clevelands House and Muskoka Wharf in Gravenhurst).

Most taking in the performance at Windsor Park, or enjoying a pleasant picnic with views of Bala Bay, likely don't notice a raised rectangular plot in the park. Although it seems completely incongruous, this unremarkable plot of elevated land has a fascinating story behind it. It is all that's left to remind us that one of Muskoka's most popular resorts that once stood on this very site.

The story of the New Windsor Hotel goes back to the earliest days of Bala when John Board built the Clifton House resort overlooking Bala Bay in 1890. This was only the second hotel in the still-young community. Interestingly, the first resort, Bala Falls Hotel, had been built by Board's brother. John Board operated the hotel for a decade before electing to move out West. He sold Clifton House to William McDivitt, who promptly renamed it the Windsor Hotel (but not the New Windsor Hotel—this will all make sense in a bit).

Business flourished, and over the next few years McDivitt proceeded to add several annexes to increase accommodation capacity. He also added a laundry and, fatefully, a gas house to provide the hotel acetylene lighting. Gas lighting was the height of luxury at the time, but also highly unstable. McDivitt would come to painfully regret the decision.

In May of 1909, the hotel burned to the ground after an acetylene explosion caused a raging fire that couldn't be checked. From the ashes of the Windsor came the New Windsor Hotel, a more modern and aesthetic hotel with the latest luxuries and room for 175 guests. McDivitt spared no expense in rebuilding but sadly hadn't learned his lesson, once again installing a highly combustible and unstable acetylene lighting. The hotel was less than a year old when a second acetylene explosion, in February 1910, killed McDivitt's eldest son, Thomas, aged 23. The resulting fire was easily contained, and the actual damage to the hotel was minimal—indeed, it was up and running by summer—but that was small solace for the grieving McDivitt family.

Life does go on; however, and both the hotel and the family flourished. Oscar McDivitt, another of McDivitt's sons, became Bala's second mayor in 1917–18 and served several more one-year terms after that. The New Windsor Hotel, meanwhile, became one of the more popular hotels in Muskoka and a familiar landmark on Bala Bay for several generations.

The McDivitt's ran the hotel well into the 1940s, but by then drastic changes in the tourism industry were rocking Muskoka's summer resorts. Seeing the writing on the wall, the family decided to sell, turning their backs on the hotel that had meant so much to their fortunes, but also cost them so dearly.

The New Windsor Hotel struggled in the post-war world and changed owners several times before closing in the early 1960s. The once-grand hotel then sat empty and increasingly derelict until it was demolished in 1969 before a large crowd of onlookers, some merely curious, others tearful locals with heavy hearts as they witnessed a part of their community's history being ripped away.

The raised rectangular plot in Windsor Park marks the foundations of this once prominent hotel and reminds us of one family's industry and heartbreak.

Guests at the Windsor Hotel

WOODCHESTER VILLA

15 King Street, Bracebridge
Admission
Web: www.bracebridge.ca/en/explore/woodchester-.aspx
Phone: 705-645-6319
Hours by Appointment or Special Event

One of the few octagonal homes still remaining in Ontario, Woodchester Villa was home to Bracebridge mill owner Henry Bird and family.

Woodchester Villa—an octagonal home-turned-museum that is nearly 150 years old—is the most unique structure in Muskoka. Nestled within a sheltered grove atop a steep, winding drive overlooking Bracebridge, the villa is seemingly removed from the modern world with its character still set in the 19th century, reflecting the life and character of its builder, Henry Bird.

The son of a prominent British textile miller, Bird followed in his father's footsteps by establishing his own mill in Peel Township, Ontario. Sadly, in 1872, Bird's wife and their two children all died of tuberculosis within weeks of each other. Inconsolable, Bird fled the scene of his heartbreak and started over again, establishing a new woollen mill—the first in Muskoka—alongside the waterfall in Bracebridge. One year later, he remarried and began planning a new home, one that reflected his status as one of Bracebridge's richest men.

Although Bird remarried and had more children, not a day went by that he didn't think of his first family and grieve his loss. The unique design of his new home was a reflection of his lingering pain and his desire to never again endure the agony of burying a loved one to tuberculosis. Bird was inspired by the writings of Orson Squire Fowler, a leading promoter of this style of construction, who stressed the benefits of octagonal homes in his book, *The Octagonal Home: A Home for All*, in which he described them inherently healthier than standard homes. Whether or not there was any truth to such claims, all seven of Bird's children from his second marriage reached adulthood without serious illness.

It would take Bird 10 years to complete this home, which bears the distinction of being one of the first poured concrete homes in Ontario, a bold and revolutionary step, and one of the largest eight-sided houses ever erected in Canada. Innovation didn't end with the home's design. Bird ensured that his home had the latest in modern amenities, many of them previously unheard of in Muskoka. Woodchester Villa was, for example, the first home in town to have a telephone, electric lighting and, in a time when most people still used outhouses and chamber pots, indoor plumbing with a water pressure system fed by rainwater storage tanks on the second floor. The Bird home also boasted forced air heating, ventilation shafts to remove stale air and a large dumb waiter designed to carry meals from the basement kitchen to the rooms above. Speaking tubes were built into the walls and connected to the kitchen, dining room and master bedroom. In short, Woodchester Villa was a showcase of modernity and forward thinking in Muskoka.

If the design of his home seemed unusual, perhaps even bizarre, to his friends and neighbours, Bird would laughingly explain that he "wanted to build a bird cage to keep my Birds in."

The largest remaining octagonal home in Ontario and one of Canada's best enduring specimens of this 19th-century style of construction, Woodchester Villa was designated a public historic site under the Ontario Heritage Act in 1979, and in 1984, achieved formal classification by the Ontario Heritage Foundation as an historic site. The former Bird home is a true Muskoka treasure.

Today the manor and the surrounding 10 acres of parkland are owned by the Town of Bracebridge, serving as a portal into the lives of the Bird family and the development of the community of which they were a vital part. The house was lavishly furnished to reflect how it might have looked around 1914, accurate down to the smallest detail. Clothing, books, furnishings, music and photographs all evoke the period with authenticity. Mrs. Bird's dress lies softly on her bed, perhaps in preparation for attending church service or a social function, and Mr. Bird's study is as he left it so many years ago. All that's missing is his presence.

Tours can be booked through the town's event coordinator. Numerous special events are held at the heritage home, including tea socials and outdoor movies held on the same spot where, once upon a time, the Birds hosted town elites for refined social functions.

Tip: Woodchester Villa whispers mystery, so why not join one of the ghost tours that explore its haunted past?

Muskoka Road Trips

Muskoka is a big region with too many sites to be seen in a single day. It's just not possible, nor would that allow you the opportunity to savour the experience. Instead, we've created a series of custom road trips for you, each one capable of being completed in an adventurous day or perhaps a more leisurely weekend.

Muskoka developed around the big four lakes (Lake Muskoka, Lake Rosseau, Lake Joseph and Lake of Bays), and so it seemed fitting to do the same when crafting these tours.

The **Lake Muskoka Tour** begins at the Gateway to Gravenhurst, where countless summer vacations have begun for 150 years, and follows a clockwise route through the postcard-worthy villages of Bala and Port Carling, before ending in Bracebridge, famed for its many waterfalls.

The **Lake Rosseau Tour** runs from Port Sandfield in the south, heads north to Rosseau, a community with oodles of charm, and across the northern shore of the lake—in one place within metres of Brackenrig Bay—back to Highway 11 and concludes with several atmospheric ghost towns.

Finally, the **North Muskoka Tour** takes you around Lake of Bays, Peninsula, Fairy and Mary Lakes to include the town of Huntsville and smaller communities such as Dorset and Baysville. It's an easy jaunt of dense forests, shimmering lakes and small-town vibes.

Regardless of the tour selected, be sure to leave some time to enjoy some of the many shops and restaurants you'll encounter along the way. From wines to fresh market goods, antiques to handicrafts, cottage wares to boutique goods, there's something for everyone.

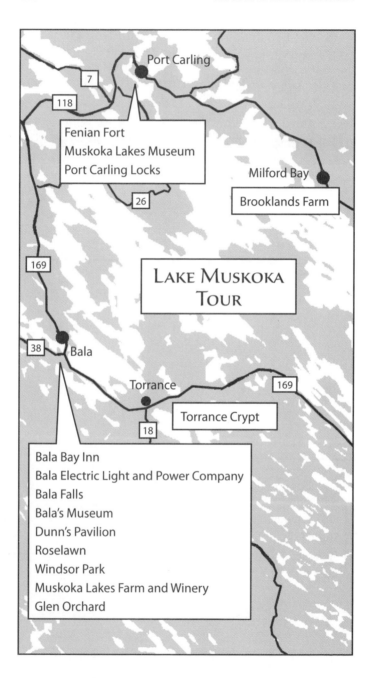

Port Carling

7

118

Fenian Fort
Muskoka Lakes Museum
Port Carling Locks

Milford Bay

26

Brooklands Farm

169

LAKE MUSKOKA
TOUR

38 Bala

Torrance

169

Torrance Crypt

18

Bala Bay Inn
Bala Electric Light and Power Company
Bala Falls
Bala's Museum
Dunn's Pavilion
Roselawn
Windsor Park
Muskoka Lakes Farm and Winery
Glen Orchard

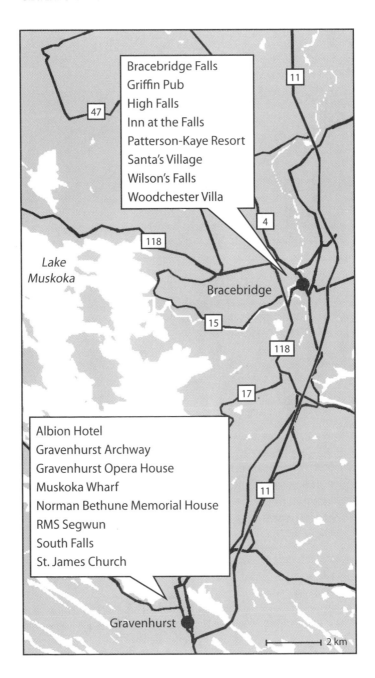

Bracebridge Falls
Griffin Pub
High Falls
Inn at the Falls
Patterson-Kaye Resort
Santa's Village
Wilson's Falls
Woodchester Villa

47

11

4

118

Lake
Muskoka

Bracebridge

15

118

17

Albion Hotel
Gravenhurst Archway
Gravenhurst Opera House
Muskoka Wharf
Norman Bethune Memorial House
RMS Segwun
South Falls
St. James Church

11

Gravenhurst

2 km

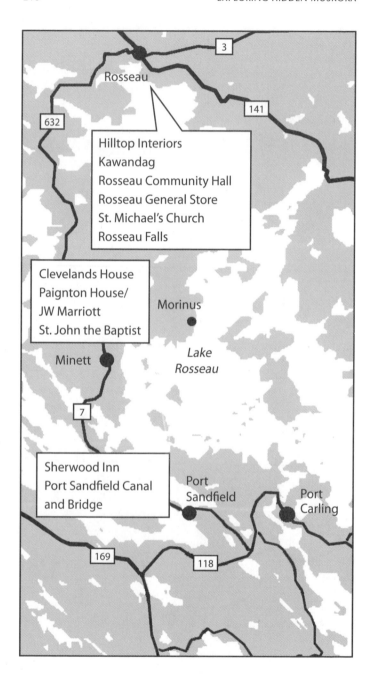

Rosseau

3

141

632

Hilltop Interiors
Kawandag
Rosseau Community Hall
Rosseau General Store
St. Michael's Church
Rosseau Falls

Clevelands House
Paignton House/
JW Marriott
St. John the Baptist

Morinus

Minett

Lake
Rosseau

7

Sherwood Inn
Port Sandfield Canal
and Bridge

Port
Sandfield

Port
Carling

169

118

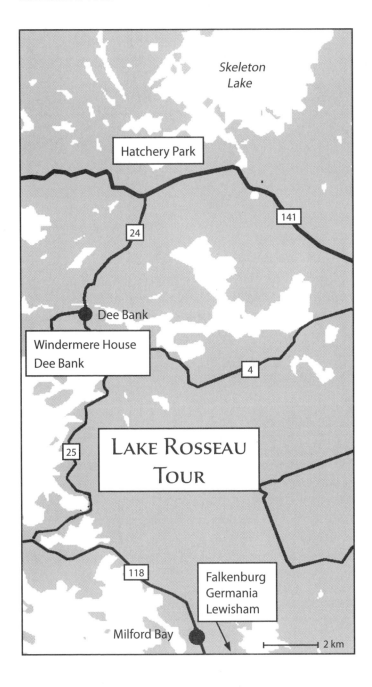

Skeleton Lake

Hatchery Park

141

24

Dee Bank

Windermere House
Dee Bank

4

LAKE ROSSEAU
TOUR

25

118

Falkenburg
Germania
Lewisham

Milford Bay

2 km

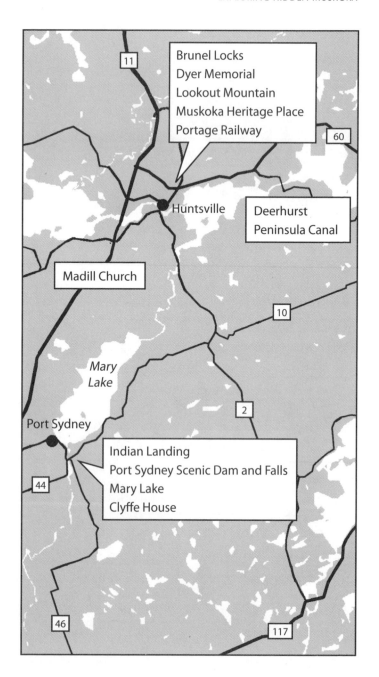

Brunel Locks
Dyer Memorial
Lookout Mountain
Muskoka Heritage Place
Portage Railway

11

60

Huntsville

Deerhurst
Peninsula Canal

Madill Church

10

Mary
Lake

2

Port Sydney

Indian Landing
Port Sydney Scenic Dam and Falls
Mary Lake
Clyffe House

44

46

117

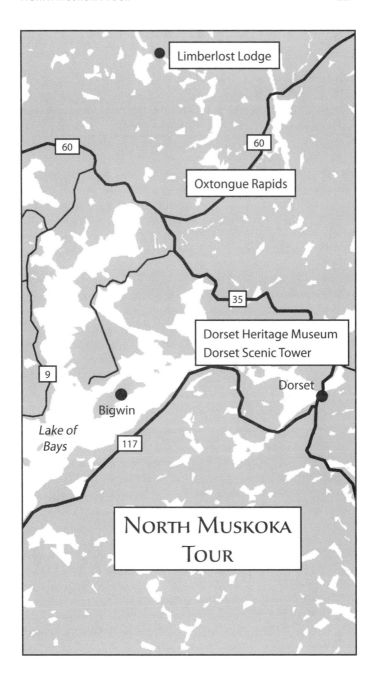

Limberlost Lodge

60

60

Oxtongue Rapids

35

Dorset Heritage Museum
Dorset Scenic Tower

Dorset

9

Bigwin

Lake of
Bays

117

North Muskoka
Tour

Notes on Sources

Boyer, Barbaranne. *Muskoka's Grand Hotels*. Erin: The Boston Mills Press, 1987.

Canadian Summer Resorts: *Illustrated Souvenir and Guide*. Toronto: F. Smily, 1900.

Coombe, Geraldine. *Muskoka Past and Present*. Toronto: McGraw-Hill Ryerson, 1976.

Cope, Leila M. *A History of the Village of Port Carling*. Bracebridge, ON: Herald-Gazette Press, 1956.

Denison, John. *Micklethwaite's Muskoka*. Erin: The Boston Mills Press, 1993.

Findlay, Mary Lynn. *Lures and Legends of Lake of Bays*. Bracebridge, 1973.

Hamilton, W.E., ed. *Guide Book and Atlas of Muskoka and Parry Sound Districts*. Toronto: H.R. Page, 1879.

Hind, Andrew and Maria Da Silva. *Ghost Towns of Muskoka*. Toronto: Dundurn, 2008.

Hind, Andrew and Maria Da Silva. *Muskoka Resorts: Then and Now*. Toronto: Dundurn, 2011.

Hind, Andrew. *Patterson-Kaye: A Celebration*. Createspace, 2016.

Hind, Andrew and Maria Da Silva. *RMS Segwun: Queen of Muskoka*. Toronto: Dundurn, 2012.

Hind, Andrew and Maria Da Silva: *Sherwood Inn: 80 Years of Tradition*. Createspace, 2018.

Hind, Andrew and Maria Da Silva. *The Summer Home of Christmas Spirit: 60 Years of Santa's Village*. Createspace, 2015.

Hosking, Carol. *Clevelands House: Summer Memories*. Erin, ON: The Boston Mills Press, 1993.

Hutton, Jack. "Bala Bay Inn gets a new lease on life." *The Muskoka Sun*. June 29, 2006.

Hutton, Jack. "Bala Bay Inn has links to poet Robert Browning." *The Muskoka Sun*. July 15, 2010.

Kennedy, Laura. *Deerhurst Resort: A Century of Hospitality in Northern Muskoka*. Erin: The Boston Mills Press, 1995.

MacLellan, Bruce. *Postcards from Lake of Bays*. Self-published, 2007.

MacLellan, Bruce. *Back Again at Lake of Bays*. Self-published, 2010.

McTaggart, Douglas. *Bigwin Inn*. Erin, ON: The Boston Mills Press, 1992.

Muskoka Lakes Association. *Summertimes: In Celebration of 100 Years of the Muskoka Lakes Association*. Erin, ON: The Boston Mills Press, 1994.

Peninsula Lake Association Historical Committee. *Pen Lake: Reflections of Peninsula Lake*. Erin, Ontario: The Boston Mills Press, 1994.

Pryke, Susan. *Explore Muskoka*. Erin, ON: The Boston Mills Press, 1987.

Pryke, Susan. *Explore Muskoka Lakes*. Erin, ON: The Boston Mills Press, 1990.

Pryke, Susan. *The History of Clevelands House: Magic Summers*. Erin, ON: The Boston Mills Press, 2001.

Pryke, Susan. *Windermere House: The Tradition Continues*. Toronto: The Boston Mills Press, 1999.

Research Committee of the Muskoka Pioneer Village. *Huntsville: Pictures from the Past*. Erin, Ontario: The Boston Mills Press, 1986.

Rice, Harmon E. *Brief Centennial History of Huntsville*. Huntsville, ON: Forester Press, 1964.

Rosseau Historical Society. *Rosseau: The Early Years*. Rosseau, ON: Rosseau Historical Society, 1999.

Rosseau Historical Sociey. *Rosseau: Then and Now*. Rosseau, ON: Rosseau Historical Society, 2004.

Sutton, Frederick William. *Early History of Bala*. Bracebridge, ON: Herald-Gazette Press, 1970.

Tatley, Richard. *The Steamboat Era in the Muskokas: Volume I— To the Golden Years*. Erin: The Boston Mills Press, 1983.

Tatley, Richard. *The Steamboat Era in the Muskokas: Volume II— The Golden Years to the Present*. Erin: The Boston Mills Press, 1983.

Taylor, Cameron. *Enchanted Summers*. Toronto: Lynx Images, 1997.

About the Author

Andrew Hind is a freelance writer who specializes in history and travel. He has a passion for bringing to light unusual stories, little-known episodes in history and fascinating locations few people know about. Andrew is the author of more than 20 books and has contributed numerous articles to national and international magazines and newspapers and conducts guided historical tours, helping people connect with the past in a personal way.

Andrew developed a love for history early on, and he hopes, through his writing, to kindle a similar passion in others. Andrew has always loved the stories behind historical places and the people that gave life to them. He has wanted to share those stories for a very long time. You can follow him on Twitter @discoveriesAM.